D1334088

Addison Wesley Longman Limited,
Edinburgh Gate,
Harlow,
Essex CM20 2JE,
United Kingdom
and Associated Companies throughout the world.

Published in the United States of America
by Addison Wesley Longman Inc. New York

First published 1999

ISBN 0-582-32721 0 PPR

Visit Addison Wesley Longman on the world wide web at http://www.awl-he.com

British Library Cataloguing-in-Publication Data
A catalogue record for this book is available from the British Library

Library of Congress Cataloging-in-Publication Data
Hutchinson, John F.
   Late Imperial Russia: 1890–1917/John F. Hutchinson.
      p.   cm. -- (Seminar studies in history)
   Includes bibliographical references and index.
   ISBN 0-582-32721-0
   1. Russia--History--Alexander III, 1881–1894. 2. Russia--History-
-Nicholas II, 1894–1917. I. Title. II. Series.
DK241.H88   1999
947.08′2--dc21
                                    98-36186
                                       CIP

Set by 7 in 10/12 Sabon
Printed in Malaysia, CLP

CONTENTS

NOTE ON REFERENCING SYSTEM

Readers should note that numbers in square brackets [5] refer them to the corresponding entry in the Bibliography at the end of the book (specific page numbers are given in italics). A number in square brackets preceded by *Doc.* [*Doc. 5*] refers readers to the corresponding item in the Documents section which follows the main text. Words and abbreviations asterisked at first occurrence are defined in the Glossary.

LIST OF MAPS

NAMES, DATES AND TRANSLITERATION

1. In the text, Russian first names have been anglicized, wherever there is an accepted English equivalent, and patronymics have been omitted. In the Guide to Characters, first names and patronymics are given in their Russian form.

2. All dates given here are Old Style, i.e. according to the Julian calendar used in Russia until 1918; in the nineteenth century, it was twelve days, and in the twentieth century, thirteen days behind the (New Style) Gregorian calendar used in Western Europe. Wherever the context requires it, dates are given in both styles.

3. Transliteration of the Cyrillic alphabet follows a modified form of the Library of Congress system, omitting soft and hard signs.

ACKNOWLEDGEMENTS

I wish to thank Gordon Martel for encouraging me in this project from the beginning; and my colleague Richard Debo, who was kind enough to read the manuscript with his fine critical eye. Any errors that remain are, of course, my own responsibility.

The publishers would like to thank the following for permission to reproduce copyright material: Edward Arnold for an extract from Martin McCauley, *Octobrists to Bolsheviks: Imperial Russia 1915–1917* (1984), pp. 71–3; Princeton University Press for an extract from W. Sablinsky, *The Road to Bloody Sunday: Father Gapon and the St Petersburg Massacre 1905* (1976), pp. 344–9, M.E. Sharpe for an extract from M. Shatz and J.E. Zimmerman, *Vehkhi/Landmarks: A Collection of Articles about the Russian Intelligensia* (1994), pp. 153–4; Stanford University Press for extracts from Reginald E. Zelnik (trans. and ed.), *A Radical Worker in Tsarist Russia* (© 1986 by the Board of Trustees of the Leland Stanford Junior University) and V.I. Gurko, *Features and Figures of the Past: Government and Opinion in the Reign of Nicholas II* (1939), pp. 60–4; The University of Michigan Press for an extract from K.P. Pobedonostsev, *Reflections of a Russian Statesman* (1965), pp. 117–21.

In memory of

Karl David Patterson, 1941–1996

AN INTRODUCTION TO THE SERIES

Such is the pace of historical enquiry in the modern world that there is an ever-widening gap between the specialist article or monograph, incorporating the results of current research, and general surveys, which inevitably become out of date. *Seminar Studies in History* are designed to bridge this gap. The series was founded by Patrick Richardson in 1966 and his aim was to cover major themes in British, European and World history. Between 1980 and 1996 Roger Lockyer continued his work, before handing the editorship over to Clive Emsley and Gordon Martel. Clive Emsley is Professor of History at the Open University, while Gordon Martel is Professor of International History at the University of Northern British Columbia, Canada and Senior Research Fellow at De Montfort University.

All the books are written by experts in their field who are not only familiar with the latest research but have often contributed to it. They are frequently revised, in order to take account of new information and interpretations. They provide a selection of documents to illustrate major themes and provoke discussion, and also a guide to further reading. The aim of *Seminar Studie*s is to clarify complex issues without over-simplifying them, and to stimulate readers into deepening their knowledge and understanding of major themes and topics.

PART ONE: THE BACKGROUND

1 RUSSIA IN THE LATE 19th CENTURY

THE EMPIRE AND ITS INHABITANTS

Late Imperial Russia was ruled by Tsar Alexander III from 1881 to 1894, and then by his son, Tsar Nicholas II, from 1894 to 1917. Both were members of the Romanov family which in 1913 celebrated 300 years as Russia's ruling dynasty. Among their illustrious forbears were Peter the Great, whose victory over the Swedes in the early eighteenth century had transformed Muscovy into one of the great powers of Europe; Catherine the Great, who sought to bring the fruits of the Enlightenment to a distant and culturally backward Russia; Alexander I, whose epic confrontation with Napoleon Bonaparte is immortalized in Tolstoi's *War and Peace*; and Alexander II, the 'tsar-liberator' who ended serfdom and revamped Russia's governing structure after defeat in the Crimean War (1853–1856) underlined the need to adapt to a rapidly changing world.

The Russian Empire was, however, even older than the Romanov dynasty. Its real founder was the notorious sixteenth-century Tsar Ivan IV 'the Terrible', who defeated Russia's former overlords, the Mongols, thereby bringing the Volga river basin under Muscovite control and opening Siberia, a land rich in both furs and minerals, to Russian exploration and exploitation. His successors continued to add territories and subject peoples, many of the latter not only non-Russians but also non-Slavs. By the time Nicholas II ascended the throne in 1894, Russia's vast empire stretched from Finland and the frozen Eurasian Arctic in the north to the subtropical shores of the Black Sea and the desert oases of Turkestan in the south; its western borders adjoined those of the German and Austro-Hungarian Empires, while its already substantial territory in eastern Asia had recently been increased at the expense of the faltering Chinese Empire. Four centuries of Russian expansion – neither constant nor unopposed, it should be noted – had, by the late nineteenth century, created the largest land empire since Genghis Khan, if not since Alexander the Great. Its aspirations were symbolized by the two cities at its extremities: St Petersburg, Peter the Great's 'window onto Europe', and Vladivostok, the 'Lord of the East'.

Like their royal predecessors, Alexander III and Nicholas II were not only tsars ('Caesars'), but also autocrats, rulers whose sovereignty was absolute; their powers were subject to neither constitutional nor institutional limitations. Among the great powers of Europe, Russia was unique both because it adhered to the eastern (Orthodox) form of Christianity, and because on the eve of the twentieth century its form of government remained an hereditary autocracy. According to the mythology that was given official expression in the Fundamental Laws and sanctified by the state Church, Russian tsars derived from God the power they wielded, and it was to God alone that they were answerable for their actions. In the past, such vast power had often been exercised in ways that smacked of tyranny and caprice, but the rituals and ceremonies of the Church earnestly sought to foster the image of a pious, dutiful and fatherly ruler whose heart was at one with his people. In this propagandistic endeavour, attention turned not to the military exploits of the many 'conqueror' tsars, but rather to the 'mostgentle' Tsar Alexis, whose mid-seventeenth century life and reign came to exert a peculiar hold upon the religious imagination and devotions of Nicholas II. At a court ball celebrating the Romanov tercentenary in 1913, for example, he and Empress Alexandra dressed in costumes appropriate to the reign of Alexis, and onlookers agreed that this exercise in anachronism appeared to bring deep feelings of joy and peace to the face of the emperor.

Nicholas may well have longed for what seemed a simpler Muscovite past precisely because the challenges that he now faced in ruling Russia seemed so much more difficult and troublesome than those faced by Tsar Alexis. For, despite Nicholas' theoretically vast powers as head of state, and his exalted position as defender of both the integrity of the Russian land and the purity of its Orthodox faith, a huge gulf separated the official mythology of autocracy from the complexities that he faced in dealing with Russian reality on a day-to-day basis. Of these, none was more striking than the empire's extraordinary ethnic diversity.

When the first reasonably reliable census was taken in 1897, many Russians learned with surprise that they had already become a minority in their own empire. Out of a total population that exceeded 122 million, less than 45 per cent were now ethnic Great Russians. True, Slavic peoples constituted a majority of the entire population; Great Russians, Belorussians, Ukrainians and Poles together formed more than 73 per cent of the total, but that statistic counted for little because these groups rarely perceived an overarching common interest. Indeed, among the Slavs, disunity was far more typical than unity. Most troublesome of all were the proudly nationalist Poles, who could not forget that a century earlier, Catherine the Great had joined Prussia and Austria in destroying the venerable Polish state and partitioning its extensive territory. Merged against their will into the Russian Empire, the Poles remained separated from the Russians not only by language and history but also by religion: the overwhelming majority were Roman Catholics. Polish Catholicism and Polish nationalism were difficult to separate; indeed, some Polish nationalists drew parallels between Christ's suffering on the cross and the pitiable fate of their own partitioned nation. By contrast, from the Russian point of view, the Poles were nothing but disloyal and untrustworthy subjects who had twice rebelled against Russian rule, first in 1830 and again in 1863. Fearing that the 'virus' of nationalism might spread from Poland to neighbouring Ukraine, the Russians attempted to stamp out the tentative efforts of Ukrainian intellectuals to assert the distinctiveness of that region's history, language, or cultural identity. The partitions of Poland also brought under Russian rule about 5 million Jews, almost all of whom lived, no longer by choice, in a specially demarcated area of the western provinces known as the Pale of Settlement. Yiddish-speaking and studiously traditional in dress and appearance, the Jews understandably sought to preserve their religion and culture against attempts to convert or assimilate them, thereby earning the hatred of antisemites, who were especially active in the western and southern Ukraine.

By the end of the nineteenth century more than a quarter of the tsar's subjects were neither Russians nor Slavs. Some 13 million were Muslims, most of whom spoke various Turkic languages, and who lived mainly in the southern regions of the empire. Another 3 million inhabitants of Russia proper, living mostly in the north, belonged to various Finnic peoples, while the administratively separate Grand Duchy of Finland had a population of 2.5 million, almost all Finns, but also including a small minority of Swedes. In addition, there were Germans (found mostly in the Baltic), Latvians, Lithuanians, Georgians, and Armenians; each of these groups constituted between 1 and 2 per cent of the entire population of the empire, and in addition there were dozens of other smaller ethnic groups, especially in the mountainous regions of the Caucasus [94]. In the late Imperial period, many important conflicts would turn on relations between Russians on the one hand, and Poles, Finns and Jews on the other; the Ukrainians found themselves in conflict with Russians, Poles, and Jews, although usually for different reasons.

If the empire's ethnic and linguistic diversity was bewilderingly complex, so was the variety of religions practiced within its boundaries. To be sure, the Orthodox Church occupied a privileged position in law, but this special status partially concealed the fact that Orthodox believers were divided into three distinct groups. Besides the majority, who followed the rites of the established religion, there were two substantial minorities: the Old Believers, descendants of those whose defiant refusal to accept seventeenth-century reforms in dogma and ritual brought upon them continuing discrimination and sporadic persecution by the state; and the Uniates, mostly peasants in the western provinces, Roman Catholics who were permitted to follow the rites of the Orthodox Church in return for acknowledging the authority of the Papacy, an arrangement devised in the seventeenth century by Catholic missionaries imbued with the religious zeal of the Counter-Reformation. In the Caucasus, the Georgians and the Armenians each had their own distinctive and ancient versions of eastern Orthodoxy. Other substantial Christian populations included the Roman Catholics of Poland and Lithuania; and the Lutherans of Finland and the Baltic provinces; in addition, there were several sects, both radical and conservative, some of them offshoots of native Orthodoxy while others derived from imported Protestantism. The smaller Christian groups were far outnumbered by the mostly Sunni Muslims, whose religious ties to the Ottoman Empire periodically gave Russians cause for concern. Finally, the empire also contained Buddhists, such as the Buriat Mongols of eastern Siberia, and small groups of pagan nature-worshippers found mostly in northern and northeastern Asia. Religion, in other words, was more likely to divide than to unite the tsar's subjects.

Some idea of what this ethnic and religious complexity could mean in practice may be obtained from two examples. In the three Baltic provinces acquired by Russia after Peter the Great's lengthy war with Sweden, the landowners – the so-called 'Baltic barons' – were German-speaking Lutherans, descendants of the northern crusading orders that had come to this area both to settle and to convert the pagan Balts and Lithuanians; the peasants who worked for them were either Lutherans or Catholics who spoke Baltic (Latvian) or Finno-Ugrian (Estonian) languages. In order to ensure that the Baltic Germans would remain loyal to Russia, the tsarist regime had welcomed them into its ruling elite without requiring that they convert to Orthodoxy, while using the tool of emancipation to force their peasants into abject economic dependence upon the landowners. In Turkestan, by contrast, where the Muslim population consisted of nomads, peasants, and townspeople, the very primitivism of the nomads was seen as 'a bulwark against Islam' by Russian officials who feared the religious fanaticism of the townspeople [25 *p. 122*]. In such varied circumstances it was next to impossible to formulate policies that could be applied consistently throughout the empire.

ECONOMIC AND SOCIAL REALITIES

One of the greatest challenges facing the tsarist regime was the fact that Russian social and economic development lagged well behind that of England, or Germany, or the United States. In this regard, the 1897 census confirmed what foreign visitors had already observed: Russia was an overwhelmingly rural country. The majority of the population, 86.6 per cent, lived in the countryside, most of them in small villages. Although Moscow had a million inhabitants and St Petersburg slightly more, there were only about a dozen other substantial cities, and few of these were located in central Russia [94]. The vast majority of rural inhabitants were peasants; between three-quarters and four-fifths of the population of the empire were either engaged in agriculture or in some way dependent upon it. Although migrating to cities, becoming industrial workers, or emigrating to southern frontier areas or to Siberia were options taken by many peasants despite the difficulties involved, the fact is that the rural population continued to grow so rapidly that those who remained constantly complained of the shortage of arable land. Despite such misery and want, and in stubborn defiance of Malthus' 'providential checks' to population growth, the peasants went on creating more mouths than the countryside could feed. Ironically, but understandably, the pressure of rising population was strongest in the most fertile, black-soil regions of central and western Russia.

Many of the peasants counted in the 1897 census had been born serfs, serfdom having survived from the Muscovite era until Tsar Alexander II embarked on a programme of 'Great Reforms' in the 1860s. Whatever its legal implications, emancipation scarcely improved – indeed some would say it worsened – the economic situation of the Russian peasant. In its wake, many peasants found themselves tilling an allotment of land that was barely able to produce a subsistence for themselves and their families, let alone to offset the redemption payments that the government had imposed in return for having compensated the landlords for parting with some of 'their' land. Especially in the forest provinces, peasants supplemented meagre incomes by resorting to handicraft production during the long winter months.

Judged by the standards of peasant agriculture elsewhere – France, for example – the land allotments of Russian peasants might well have been sufficient, perhaps more than sufficient, if only they had been worked in a more efficient manner. Striking early photographs of peasants holding wooden rakes and shovels attest to the relatively primitive agricultural methods that still prevailed throughout much of rural Russia. Understanding little or nothing about fertilizers or crop rotation, most peasants employed traditional scratch ploughing methods that virtually guaranteed low yields per sown acre. Moreover, because so much of the land was periodically redistributed among members of the village commune,* peasants had little reason to think of the long-term productivity of any particular allotment. For centuries, their peasant forbears had coped with the hardships of the Russian climate and the deficiencies of soil quality by continually seeking more land to bring under the plough; hence the persistent calls in the late Imperial period that still more land be made available for peasant cultivation.

Russia's rural population grew steadily enough to maintain its proportion of the whole, no mean feat in a period when some urban areas were achieving spectacular growth rates. Urban population doubled in the thirty years before the 1897 census, and continued to increase steadily until the outbreak of war in 1914. Multi-ethnic Odessa, the principal grain export port on the Black Sea; Kharkov and Rostov-on-Don, the main southern centres of heavy industry; Baku, the oil production and distribution centre on the Caspian Sea; these and several other cities experienced phenomenal growth in the late nineteenth century. Such rapid growth put pressure on rudimentary municipal institutions that were everywhere struggling, not often successfully, with the attendant problems of urban modernization. Contemporaries found the streets of Russian cities teeming with 'vagrants, paupers, idlers, parasites, and hooligans' [23 *p. 1*], a situation which in Moscow produced systematic efforts to discipline the common people through stricter poor relief measures [59]. However, despite this recent and dramatic urban growth, Russia was still, on the eve of the twentieth century, a largely agricultural and peasant country [40].

In matters of health Russia also lagged behind the West. Mortality rates in the late nineteenth-century Russian Empire were appreciably higher than those in Western Europe or the United States. Regional differences were apparent in the statistics: rates were lower in the Baltic, the western and southwestern provinces than in central Russia, and the lower Volga provinces had the highest rates of all. Until the 1880s, urban death rates generally exceeded rural, but in St Petersburg, reputedly the unhealthiest capital in Europe, mortality rates remained startlingly high as late as 1913 [20]. Epidemiological reconstruction reveals that children accounted for a high proportion of all deaths and, more surprisingly, that there were significant differences in death rates according to religion: 'Orthodox babies perished at roughly twice the rate of Jewish infants', and were much more vulnerable than babies born into Lutheran, Catholic or Muslim families, a disparity attributable largely to differences in breast-feeding and weaning practices [76]. That Russia lagged behind Europe is clear from the fact that most deaths were still from infectious diseases. Children died mainly from measles, scarlet fever, diphtheria, and pertussis; adults from smallpox, cholera, typhus, typhoid fever, malaria and tuberculosis. The lower Volga provinces, especially Astrakhan, and the Black Sea coast were particularly vulnerable to epidemics of malaria. Because of overcrowding and poor ventilation, respiratory and eye diseases flourished during the winter months, while summer water shortages especially in the south often produced gastro-intestinal disorders. Migrating peasants and pilgrims helped to spread tuberculosis, typhus and venereal diseases. A modest downward trend in mortality rates is apparent by 1900, but whether it is attributable to better nourishment, as some have argued, or to rising standards of education and literacy reinforced by the efforts of physicians and sanitarians, remains an unsettled question [52].

REFORMERS AND REVOLUTIONARIES

By the late nineteenth century, the Russian tsar usually exercised his ostensibly unlimited powers through certain established officials and institutions. The chief executive officers of the Russian autocracy were the commanders of the army and the fleet; the ministers, appointed and dismissed by the will of the tsar; and the provincial governors, who were both the tsar's personal representatives and the executive heads of the provincial administrations [92]. Separate arrangements prevailed in the Grand Duchy of Finland and in the Cossack territories. Except in Finland, there were no legislative or representative bodies comparable with the English House of Commons or the American Congress. The Committee of Ministers, by no stretch of the imagination a unified cabinet, might at the tsar's behest consider and advise on particular measures or general matters, but neither it, nor the State Council, a largely honorific deliberative body composed of senior officials appointed by the tsar, had the power to initiate legislation or indeed to block any specific measure or course of action that found favour with the ruler. The Governing Senate, founded by Peter the Great to run the country while he made war, had long since become the senior judicial body of the empire; it registered decrees, tried to ensure consistency in the application of law, and sent out officials commissioned to enquire into local abuses, a practice that was hilariously satirized in Gogol's *The Government Inspector.*

Although the provincial towns portrayed in Russian literature appeared full of obsequious, corrupt, idle and incompetent bureaucrats, the empire was probably overgoverned at the centre and undergoverned at the local level. Too many matters required reference to St Petersburg, where the decision-making apparatus was plagued by delay, incomprehension, and a lack of co-ordinated policy. Because ministers reported separately to the tsar, there was no certain means by which overlapping or contradictory policies could be identified and reconsidered. Not until the 1860s did the empire have a co-ordinated annual budget, and even at the turn of the present century the Ministries of Finance and Interior clashed repeatedly over various aspects of domestic, especially labour, policy [114, 118]. From 1864, after considerable discussion about whether the empire needed more or fewer bureaucrats, new institutions of local government known as zemstvos* were created in the provinces and districts of European Russia, supplementing rather than replacing the local administrative apparatus overseen by the governors. Zemstvo institutions were promoted by reformers who sought to encourage responsible elements of the population to take part in local government, but the reformers' influence on Tsar Alexander II (1855–1881) was undermined by a major uprising in Poland in 1863; consequently, the zemstvos were established with fewer powers, smaller fields of jurisdiction, and under closer bureaucratic supervision than originally planned. When serf emancipation was still in the offing, some gentry landowners had sought, as compensation, a greater role for themselves in the government of the empire; most St Petersburg bureaucrats reacted strongly against such power-sharing at the national level. If the gentry could be lured into a preoccupation with local zemstvo affairs, then the bureaucrats would be free to deal with national issues, which in practice meant that they could continue to run the empire as they saw fit.

Many Russians, including some highly-placed enlightened bureaucrats, had expected rather more extensive reforms. In general, they hoped that the regime would enthusiastically encourage local self-government, not only in the countryside but also in the cities; that there would be a clear separation between the courts and the bureaucracy, so that officials would come to appreciate the need for responsible conduct within the law; that the importance of rank and estate (*soslovie**) as principles of social organization would decline in favour of more rational criteria; and that the allegedly baneful influence of the Orthodox Church, particularly in the field of education, would be reduced by a deliberate policy of secularization. Although some limited progress was made in most of these areas between 1861 and 1873, nothing like the fundamental transformation sought by some reformers was in fact achieved, or even set in motion. The tsar himself soon lost faith in the regime's ability to control the process of reform, and those who had something to lose were profoundly shaken by the Polish uprising, by the spectre of revolutionary activity in St Petersburg, and by the alarming popularity of nihilist, socialist, and even anarchist views among the younger generation.

Young Russians, especially those who were university students in the late 1860s and early 1870s, sought transformations far more drastic than those contemplated by even the most ardent reformers. Inspired by teachers who contrasted the privileges of the elite with the sufferings of the peasant population, thousands of populist students (*narodniki**) descended on the countryside in the summer of 1873, hoping to expiate their feelings of guilt by helping the allegedly instinctive socialism of the Russian peasantry to reach a new level of social and political consciousness. This 'going to the people' was, in practical terms, a fiasco; peasants reacted with indifference, suspicion, or outrage, and many narodniki beat hasty retreats, only to fall into police custody. A series of group trials and exemplary sentences followed, the regime being too shortsighted to resist punishments that were certain to convert naivete into a kind of martyrdom. The next wave of potential recruits to the revolutionary cause broke upon the shoals of reality: those who judged such grand gestures futile opted for a longer, slower road to social change by working for the zemstvos as agronomists, statisticians, and physicians; a smaller number, who believed that the populist ideology was at fault, emigrated to Geneva where, under the leadership of George Plekhanov they formed the first Marxist study group, called Emancipation of Labour; the most impatient, not more than a few dozen, convinced themselves that they could ignite the spark of revolution by terrorizing state officials, above all the emperor himself [83].

When, after a systematic campaign of terrorism, Alexander II was assassinated on 1 March, 1881 by revolutionaries calling themselves 'the People's Will', privileged society took fright. Although some argued that further revolutionary action could only be prevented by an even stronger commitment to reform, conservatives denounced as senseless the idea that the regime ought to encourage public initiatives outside bureaucratic control, such as the participation of unofficial 'outsiders' in political debate, or the discussion of political issues in the press. All such concessions, they claimed, would simply encourage those who sought to dismantle the empire and destroy the established social order. Even the carefully controlled reforms that had already been introduced now seemed at risk. As for the terrorists, five were executed and dozens of others imprisoned and sent into exile. Ironically but inevitably, their bloody triumph had stunned all Russians, producing an outpouring of sympathy for the Imperial family and discrediting revolutionary activism for more than a decade.

THE IMPERIAL REGIME AND ITS CRITICS

Succeeding his father in these appalling circumstances, Alexander III brought to the task of ruling Russia a limited number of fixed beliefs to which he clung doggedly throughout his reign. Of these, the most important was a conviction that the future greatness of Russia was his responsibility. Neither a deep nor an imaginative thinker, he reduced complex issues to simple, easily grasped polarities: strength and weakness, loyalty and disloyalty, courage and cowardice. Yet the most frequently encountered judgement of him, as a towering bulwark of reaction, is misleading: it obscures his conviction that the greatness of Russia could not now be maintained without embarking on a programme of rapid industrialization that necessarily demanded keeping the empire constantly at peace. Despite his own discomfort with change and inveterate suspicion of reform, Alexander III nevertheless headed a regime that brought much of both to Russia, albeit with little trace of enthusiasm on the part of the tsar himself. If there was idealism, it was apparent not in Finance Minister Sergei Witte's extravagant visions of what capitalist industrialization would do for Russia, but rather in the regime's enduring conviction that merely by making a few small adjustments, it could continue to rely on the loyalty of both peasants and nobles despite the changes it was bringing to the world around them.

Many of the laws enacted during the first decade of Alexander's reign were aimed at curbing what he and most of his advisers regarded as the forces of weakness, disloyalty, and cowardice. The main targets, predictably, were conspirators and propagandists who engaged in unlawful political activity, outspoken newspaper editors, university professors and students, and (especially rural) schoolteachers. From the point of view of the Ministry of the Interior, which was charged with maintaining the internal security of the state, not only did such people often and impertinently assume a right to discuss and make recommendations on matters of state policy, but they also encouraged the lower orders of society to criticize the government, and sometimes even to defy it. In order to strengthen the regime's ability to deal with real or apprehended disorder, extraordinary measures were introduced in August, 1881. Cities or even entire provinces could be declared as in a state of 'reinforced security' or, more extremely, 'extraordinary protection'; once so designated, city prefects or provincial governors were given extraordinary powers to search, arrest, fine, and deport individuals; to limit or ban gatherings of any kind; and to interfere with, or even close down, the work of zemstvo institutions. Itself an extraordinary measure, this allegedly temporary law was never approved by the State Council, nor could actions taken under its special powers be appealed to the Senate; throughout the late Imperial period it was constantly criticized, and not only by enemies of the regime, as the most flagrant example of administrative caprice. A year later, another supposedly temporary law tightened control over editors of newspapers and journals, while making it more difficult to distribute or sell publications that were in any way critical of the government. A new University Statute introduced in 1884 completely destroyed the fairly substantial autonomy that students, professors, and administrators had enjoyed for twenty years. All types of appointments, as well as the content of the curriculum, were now subject to ministerial authority, backed by carefully selected 'public trustees'; student uniforms were revived, and extensive disciplinary authority given to a new appointed official, the inspector of students. To curb disloyalty in the schoolroom, new controls were imposed on schools operated by zemstvos, the Church was encouraged to open more parish schools, and the notorious 1887 'Circular on Cooks' Children' erected administrative and financial barriers to discourage children from the lower orders from bettering their condition through education.

After imposing so many restrictions on the activities of those individuals and institutions which the autocracy regarded as suspect, it was natural for the regime to give special recognition to the supposed loyalty of peasants and nobles. The hundredth anniversary of Catherine II's 1785 Charter to the Nobility provided Alexander III with an occasion for bolstering the flagging self-esteem of nobles by urging them to play leading roles in the army, in local administration, and even in popular education, the last no doubt so as to ensure that the people were taught to accept and reaffirm the traditional social structure. An 1889 law establishing rural officials called Land Captains brought new career opportunities for the nobility; if selected for this position by the governor and approved by the Ministry of the Interior, a nobleman could exercise substantial administrative, judicial, and police authority over the peasants in his district. These new petty officials enabled the Ministry of the Interior to assert the authority of government in the villages to a degree that was unprecedented in Russian history. Creation of the Land Captains also permitted the regime to erode still further the reforms of the 1860s: in most rural areas, the new officials effectively replaced the elected justices of the peace provided for in the 1864 judicial reform, while the separate sphere of jurisdiction assigned to the Land Captains enabled the regime to dispense with earlier plans to create zemstvos at the cantonal (*volost**) level. Thus, instead of all rural inhabitants in a given area meeting together to discuss local common interests, the regime chose to reinforce the separate position of the peasants.

To be sure, peasants were not alone in being subjected to closer bureaucratic control. In 1890, local government was reordered, first by a revised Zemstvo Statute, followed in 1892 by a revised Municipal Statute. The 1890 law restricted the franchise and fixed artificial quotas to ensure noble dominance in zemstvo assemblies, while curbing the autonomy and scope for initiative not only of zemstvo employees, but even of zemstvo presidents, whose election now had to be approved by the Minister of the Interior. The 1892 law imposed analogous restrictions on municipal government. These measures were once seen as proof of the regime's determination to control social tensions and political dissent, but greater emphasis is now placed on the increasing efforts of the Interior Ministry, faced with the steady expansion of zemstvo activity, to enlarge its sphere of influence and increase its authority throughout the empire as well as in St Petersburg itself [34, 115].

It would, however, be foolish to reduce the history of late Imperial Russia to a tug-of-war between a reactionary regime and its liberal or radical opponents. In the first place, neither the servants of the tsarist regime nor their opponents were anything like as unified in their opinions, motives, and tactics as the tug-of-war image suggests. On all large issues there was a considerable variety of opinion within and across ministries, among provincial governors, and among the tsar's official and unofficial advisers. Contradictory policies flourished simultaneously. Wittingly or not, by promoting railway development and the growth of industry, Alexander III's government did at least as much to encourage as to restrict social and political change. As events elsewhere would demonstrate only too clearly, there was no innate incompatibility between urbanization and industrialization on the one hand, and authoritarian rule on the other. Russian monarchists proved remarkably ingenious when confronted by potentially unruly urban workers, and at least as adaptable as those who claimed to speak on behalf of the workers. The truth is that the opponents of tsarism, whether liberal or radical, were often no more in tune with, let alone in control of, the social dynamics at work in the country than were the policemen in the Ministry of the Interior. Some examples will underline the point. Both the policemen and the liberals mistakenly believed the zemstvos to be in a state of permanent conflict with the bureaucracy, but despite a record of substantial co-operation their beliefs at times became self-fulfilling prophecies. Urban mass politics might conceivably have led to growing support for social democracy, but in Russia popular antisemitism and protofascism were also real possibilities. Similarly, the appearance of professional groups could strengthen the social basis of liberalism, but professionals might also be ready to serve authoritarian governments, whether tsarist or (later) Bolshevik. In short, before entering the world of late Imperial Russia, it is best to check ideological and prescriptive sociological baggage at the door.

PART TWO: DESCRIPTIVE ANALYSIS

2   THE 1890s: HUNGER SETS THE AGENDA

THE FAMINE OF 1891-92

The defining event of the decade was the great famine that began in 1891, compounded the next year by epidemics of cholera and typhus that returned in 1893. Sixteen provinces of European Russia were the most severely affected by the famine, and the overall loss of life is estimated at more than a third of a million people. Nature produces crop failures, but it takes human action to turn them into famines. In this case, the endemic poverty of rural Russia had been exacerbated by the deliberately harsh grain requisitioning policies pursued by Witte's predecessor, Finance Minister Ivan Vyshnegradskii, whose tough 'export or die' approach to maintaining the value of the ruble on world markets left many peasants with less than a bare subsistence, and insufficient seed grain to survive a crop failure. The famine affected not only peasants, who lost family members as well as valuable livestock, but all those who serviced agricultural settlements, such as blacksmiths and rural traders; the dockworkers of Odessa, with no ships to load because of the sudden ban on grain exports, inevitably fell victims to unemployment.

An impending crisis was apparent in the Volga region and the black-earth provinces early in the year, and by May, it was clear that a major famine was looming. Initial efforts at relief quickly revealed not only the magnitude of the disaster, but also the formidable difficulties faced by those who sought to save the peasants from starvation and the agricultural economy from total collapse. In order to make the best use of limited transport facilities, a temporary 'dictator' was appointed to run the railways, while a Special Committee on Famine Relief (chaired by the Tsarevich, the future Nicholas II) sought to arouse, expand, and above all co-ordinate private charitable efforts in the stricken provinces, which were directed especially at helping those ineligible for government food loans. Soup kitchens, the most famous of them operated by the writer Leo Tolstoi, were set up everywhere. Two special lotteries authorized by Alexander III raised the bulk of the relief funds, used to provide seed grain and fodder as well as food (which came mainly from the unaffected provinces), and to make available at discount prices more than 40,000 replacement horses to those who had lost draft animals. These programmes were directed by the committee's energetic manager (and future Minister of the Interior), Viacheslav Plehve. If the government's temporary public works programme for the unemployed was a failure, its seed loan programme was not; when coupled with the more benign weather of 1893, it enabled the peasants who survived to produce a rich harvest, despite an overall reduction in sown area. Without minimizing the sufferings of those who endured the famine, the situation might have been considerably worse: far more people might have starved to death, and complete economic collapse could well have ensued. What is surprising is not the occurrence of famine, but rather that its potential for total disaster was kept within bounds by a regime not known for rapid or effective social intervention [91].

To be sure, many of the difficulties encountered by those organizing famine relief were, like the famine itself, largely of the government's own making. The single biggest obstacle to reaching stricken peasant households was the fact that neither the state administration nor the zemstvos operated at the lowest, cantonal (volost) level. The government, having shelved the original plans for elected cantonal zemstvos, had then created the Land Captains, many of whom were just finding their feet – and probably their cantons as well – when they were suddenly called upon to play a major role in local famine relief. Co-operation with existing provincial and district zemstvo institutions was imperative, but not so easily achieved in the wake of the 1890 Zemstvo Statute, the thrust of which rankled the very people on whom the government was now forced to lean. Only such a huge task, such an imminent danger, could have brought together officials of the provincial bureaucracy, cocky but inexperienced Land Captains, resentful zemstvo members, and cautious but desperate peasant elders. Forced and uncomfortable though their co-operation may have been, the fact that it happened at all led some participants and observers to anticipate a change of heart on the part of a government that appeared to have set itself against extending public participation in local self-government.

In the wake of the famine, Russians hastened to assign responsibility and draw lessons. Some blamed the predatory taxes levied by the government; others argued that communal land tenure was the real villain, and that achieving rural prosperity demanded abolition of the village communes. For many prosperous Russians who volunteered their help to distribute relief supplies in the countryside, the experience was an eye-opener; not only did they learn first-hand about rural poverty, but also about the remarkable willingness of the very poor to share their last scraps of food with passing beggars. Not everyone regarded these ad hoc relief efforts as praiseworthy. One prominent charity reformer condemned 'carelessly distributed alms' for increasing the number of beggars; since both zemstvos and peasant communes neglected poor relief, he continued, what Russia needed were special agencies of public assistance, comparable to England's Poor Law Guardians [59 p. 79].

The epidemics of cholera and typhus that had accompanied the famine left a legacy that was larger than the death toll itself. Physicians in zemstvo employment had already crossed swords with elected zemstvo deputies, many of whom were unwilling to spend money on programmes of sanitary education and regulation. Now that the causative organism and method of transmission of cholera had been established, physicians saw no reason why they should defer to the wishes of those who knew less than they did about how to prevent disease. Moreover, in a climate of popular ignorance, rumours flourished; some hotheads claimed that the government had deliberately caused the epidemic in order to reduce the numbers of the poor, and that physicians and officials were their accomplices. In some parts of the country, frenzied mobs attacked medical personnel, and physicians began to fear for their lives; their fears only increased when the army's heavy-handed suppression of popular disturbances convinced rioters that the rumours were indeed correct. Physicians concluded that education, not brute force, was the only way to stop such reactions in future, but effective preventive and educational programmes could be mounted only if government officials and zemstvo deputies were willing to grant autonomy to properly organized sanitary commissions. A desirable model was already to be found in the more enlightened arrangements that prevailed in the Moscow provincial zemstvo [37]. Conflicts such as this, in which expertise challenged officialdom, would become more common throughout the late Imperial period.

THE TRANS-SIBERIAN RAILROAD

Before the full extent of the famine crisis was known, the tsar announced (March, 1891) his decision to build a railway linking European Russia with Siberia and its Pacific possessions. The idea of a railroad across Siberia was not new, but the project was so dauntingly large, risky, and expensive that successive ministers of finance, especially the ultra-cautious Vyshnegradskii, had consistently opposed it. However, Alexander III, sensibly worried that other powers might take advantage of the weakness of Russian control beyond the Urals and especially in the far east, wished to see the railroad built quickly.

He found an enthusiastic supporter of the project in his recently appointed Minister of Transport, Sergei Witte, ironically the former director of the railways department of the Ministry of Finance. Opposition to building the railroad came not only from fiscal but also political conservatives, who claimed that encouraging peasants to colonize Siberia would deplete the cheap labour supply upon which noble landlords had come to depend, and from traditionalists (at both ends of the political spectrum) who deplored the invasion of the Russian countryside by the alien, westernizing forces of industrialization. Supporters countered with arguments that emphasized international strategic and military considerations, held up railroads (and technology in general) as the engine of large-scale economic growth, envisioned reducing the problem of overpopulation by creating new settlements on virgin land, and insisted that drawing Siberia closer to the rest of the empire would arrest the growth of a regional, perhaps even secessionist, outlook. These conflicts continued long after the Tsarevich laid the first stone in Vladivostok, but eventually the supporters of 'taming the wild east' triumphed [*66 p. 141*].

After Vyshnegradskii retired in disgrace in the summer of 1892, Witte was appointed Minister of Finance. Perceived by snobs in St. Petersburg as a hard-headed but uncultured businessman, Witte was nevertheless capable of eulogizing Russia's 'mission of cultural enlightenment', enticing the sincerely devout Tsar with visions of Orthodox Russia, rather than Western Europe, as the bearer of 'the principles of Christian enlightenment – in the Asiatic East' [*Doc. 1*]. This remarkably unqualified enthusiasm even led him to hope that international trade would soon be rerouted via the Siberian railroad, theoretically a shorter route between east and west than the Suez canal.

Such extravagant dreams bore little relation to the task at hand. The chosen route involved building more than 4,000 miles of track, not only traversing the great rivers of Siberia, but also penetrating the extremely challenging mountainous region east of Irkutsk. With more than 150 million rubles unexpectedly consumed by famine relief, and domestic producers already promised artificially high returns for supplying the necessary rails and rolling stock, the strictest economy was essential. Under orders from the tsar that the railway be built as cheaply as possible, engineers and designers cut every possible corner. Construction methods arguably more suited to a fairground than a transcontinental railway were adopted, ostensibly in order to keep costs low, but not surprisingly they produced a distinctly inferior result, and in any case actual expenses significantly outran the original estimates. The track bed could withstand only three trains a day in either direction, and many stations were located inconveniently far from the towns they were meant to serve. Even in 1901, when the railway was, somewhat prematurely, declared finished, Lake Baikal still had to be crossed by ferry; completion of an additional line along its southern shore took several more years. True, the railway project led to important discoveries – gold being the most welcome – of the mineral wealth of Siberia, and to schemes for peasant resettlement. Between 1892 and 1902, almost a million peasants boarded the railway to begin new lives, mostly in western Siberia. On balance, however, current thinking holds that 'the economic advantages the railroad brought to Siberia were questionable and its cost was indefensible under the circumstances' [66 p. 222].

Even more questionable were the alleged strategic benefits to be gained. Its very construction was perceived by the Japanese as both a military threat to their own country, and as an indication of Russia's intention to infiltrate and eventually annex Manchuria; the prospect of its completion certainly played a part in provoking Japan's short, victorious war with China (1894–95). When Russia later negotiated with the Chinese railway concessions that permitted a direct route across Manchuria to Vladivostok (Chinese Eastern Railway, 1896), and a South Manchurian branch line from Kharbin (Harbin) to Port Arthur, Japanese fears seemed more than justified. Ironically, when war with Japan finally came in 1904, it was the Russians who suffered most from their own cheeseparing economies. Marginally functional at the best of times, this substandard railway was almost paralyzed by the extraordinary demands of war.

NICHOLAS THE UNREADY

Alexander III did not live to see the Trans-Siberian railway completed, or even to celebrate his fiftieth birthday. Sickening quite suddenly in January, 1894, he died before the year was out. Russians were understandably shocked because his hitherto robust health and exceptional strength were almost legendary. When the royal train was wrecked in an accident, for example, the tsar had used his own body to prevent a metal roof from collapsing while family members escaped. Premature death was the last thing expected of a ruler whose physical presence – bulky, solid and firm – had come to personify the autocracy itself. No one was more appalled by Alexander's death than his heir, Grand Duke Nicholas Alexandrovich, who now succeeded his father as Nicholas II. An immature, even innocent, twenty-six year old, well-tutored but with little experience of affairs of state, Nicholas was utterly dismayed at the prospect of becoming tsar [60]. True, he had been sent on a world tour and had chaired the Special Committee on Famine Relief, but he was much more at ease on parade grounds and in officers' messes than in the corridors of power in St Petersburg. Until his father's imminent death became a horrifying possibility, Nicholas had expected nothing more taxing in his immediate future than the splendid ceremony that would celebrate his marriage to Princess Alix of Hesse-Darmstadt. The actual wedding ceremony, held only weeks after the funeral, was a far more sombre affair, scarcely a respite from the obligatory period of official mourning. Fate may have thrust a reluctant Nicholas on to the throne, but reluctance should not be confused with weakness; his own father's reign proved that strength of character and force of will could overcome the appalling circumstances of a sudden accession.

What sort of autocrat the young Nicholas would make was a matter of great concern to his advisers, particularly his former tutor, Constantine Pobedonostsev who, as Procurator-General of the Holy Synod,* was the lay head of the Orthodox Church. A professor of civil and constitutional law with an impressive knowledge of what might today be called comparative government, Pobedonostsev was an ultra-conservative in his political views [Doc. 2]. Like Dostoevskii's *Grand Inquisitor*, for whom he may have been the model, Pobedonostsev's view of human nature was extremely pessimistic. He believed that the main task of those in authority was not to promote some chimerical 'greatest good', but rather to keep human beings from utterly destroying themselves through their own vice and wickedness. Well read if not well travelled, he reserved his greatest venom for democracy, which he called 'the greatest falsehood of our time' [10], and for the press, which he believed capable of vulgarizing if not destroying the moral values of civilized society. With greater perspicacity than most of his contemporaries in the West, Pobedonostsev exposed the underlying weakness of representative government, the inevitable moral bankruptcy of mass politics, and the shameless behaviour of the popular press. From his perspective, the Russian Empire was fortunate: although already beset from several directions, it had not yet been irredeemably corrupted. The autocracy, the Church, the peasantry in its village communities: for him these were unique national institutions to be lovingly preserved and vigorously defended against enemies who marched under the banners of individualism, liberalism, and democracy [28]. In Russia these enemies would be found among the educated, especially the educated aristocrats, for whom the intellectual world of Western Europe seemed to hold an irresistible attraction.

In the early days of Alexander III's reign, Pobedonostsev had helped to strengthen the monarch's resolve to defend the autocracy against those who counselled reform, and his continuing influence on the tsar is apparent, for example, in the limitations placed on the activities of zemstvos and municipalities. Whenever it was a matter of putting the interests of Russians ahead of non-Russians, or of bolstering the position of the Orthodox Church, or of devising further restrictions on the Jewish population, Pobedonostsev always found Alexander III innately sympathetic. Yet his influence on the tsar fell well short of that of an *eminence grise*. Deeply hostile to cabinet government, he himself valued and defended the autocrat's separate relationship with each of his ministers, regardless of the fact that it inevitably limited his own influence. In any case, this ruler was perfectly capable of ignoring Pobedonostsev's views when, for example, his own perception of Russia's national interest led him to approve a diplomatic alliance with republican France, or to encourage the headlong pace of industrialization promoted by Witte. With Nicholas II now on the throne, observers wondered whether Pobedonostsev's influence might not increase; after all, his participation in affairs of state dated back to the reign of Alexander II, and the uncertain young ruler might need an experienced navigator.

Finance Minister Witte, who had a huge stake in maintaining the continuity of state economic policy, was equally interested in sizing up the abilities and intelligence of the young emperor. Although Witte agreed with Pobedonostsev about both the uniqueness of Russia and the importance of maintaining the autocracy, they disagreed about much else. Where Pobedonostsev would have preferred to preserve Russia by, as it were, petrifying it in amber, Witte enthusiastically promoted change. In his view, only by rushing to catch up with the Industrial Revolution could the autocracy, and therefore the Russian Empire, hope to survive. In 1890, Russia was the least industrialized of all the great powers, and in Witte's opinion its reach had come dangerously close to exceeding its grasp. In order to catch up as quickly as possible with Europe, Great Britain and the United States, Russia would have to achieve phenomenal rates of industrial growth. To do so would in turn require a sweeping transformation of Russian habits, customs, and beliefs: attitudes to authority, work, time, discipline, and vodka consumption (to mention only the most obvious) would all have to change as part of the process of industrialization [*Doc. 3*]. So also would the suspicion and fear, mingled with contempt, which most educated Russians – whether conservative landowners or populist intellectuals – reserved for those engaged in commercial and industrial activity. It was a tall order.

Witte probably understood more about the obstacles to industrialization than he did about where Russia would be led if those obstacles were removed. His vision of Russia's economic future was borrowed from the theories of the German economist Friedrich List: use the power and resources of the state to promote a railroad boom, which would foster, in sequence, the growth of heavy industry, then of light industry, then of greater prosperity in urban areas, and finally greater prosperity in rural areas. High tariffs, heavy foreign investment, and a stable currency that was convertible on world markets were all parts of Witte's programme, as was his deliberate boosting of industrial and technological development and education by, for example, special exhibitions, prizes and other promotional devices. Above all, Witte hoped to see the emergence of a class of entrepreneurs possessed of an exciting sense of vision, driven by a dynamism yet to be seen in Russia, and rewarded not only by the growth of profits but also by the challenge of weighing and managing risks.

Witte was once regarded as a figure of near-heroic proportions, a veritable Peter the Great, who almost single-handedly battled indifference and obscurantism to bring Russia into the modern age [114]. More recent scholarship has questioned the components of his 'system', and consistently scaled down earlier evaluations of his personal responsibility for the economic boom that Russia enjoyed during the 1890s. Some stress his debt to earlier ministers of finance who had encouraged railroad development and attracted foreign investors by stabilizing the currency and producing export surpluses [94]. The extremely high tariff of 1891, introduced by Vyshnegradskii, was a vital component of the industrial boom that lasted until the end of the decade. Whether the Trans-Siberian railway, the emblem of Witte's programme, helped to teach Russians anything about managerial capitalism has been questioned, as has the centrality of railroad development to the industrialization and modernization of Russia [66]. Witte himself, after leaving the Finance Ministry, recognized and lamented the fact that a policy of state leadership seemed to have accustomed too many Russian businessmen to expect that the state would always lead. Both the weaknesses and the strengths of his economic programme derived from its ultimate political purpose, the salvation of the autocracy. Yet would the hesitant new emperor continue to support a programme that demanded so much from so many, and was therefore vulnerable to criticism from all sides?

In the event, Nicholas made no immediate changes in the policies or personnel that he inherited from his father. Lacking an established political identity of his own, he felt most secure in clinging to the *status quo*, although it is doubtful whether at this stage he grasped the enormous challenges to established patterns and customs that were essential parts of Witte's programme. What did become clear very early on, however, was the young monarch's lack of appreciation for the sensibilities of his subjects, especially those, ironically, who linked the security of their own future to the fortunes of the dynasty. For loyal monarchists, the coronation of a tsar was an important symbolic moment of religious dedication and national affirmation, but in Nicholas' case the solemnity of the occasion was overshadowed by disaster: a huge crowd assembled at Khodynka field (on the outskirts of Moscow) for the traditional distribution of coronation keepsakes suddenly panicked and stampeded, resulting in the loss of well over 1,300 lives [*Doc. 4*]. Some asked what responsibility the police bore for improperly controlling the movements of more than half a million people, but far more were aghast on learning that the emperor and empress that very night attended a grand ball at the French embassy. True, Nicholas bore no personal responsibility for the disaster, which seems to have been the product of bureaucratic bungling and infighting, and he went most unwillingly to the ball, having been persuaded by advisers that his absence would grievously offend Russia's newest ally. Nevertheless, the Khodynka tragedy created a literally disastrous first impression from which Nicholas was never able to make a complete escape [60]. Further discomfiting evidence of the tsar's capacity for giving needless offence came in the following year, when he labelled as 'senseless dreams' the humbly expressed desire of a dozen zemstvo assemblies that in future 'the voice of the zemstvo would be allowed to reach the heights of the throne' [65 p. 140]. So timid and deferential a request scarcely merited this stinging rebuke, an early sign that Nicholas' political judgement might be less than astute. No doubt the tsar believed that he was demonstrating his resolve to be a worthy successor to his father. Nevertheless, these ill-considered words were often discussed and much criticized; together with the bad impression created by the Khodynka disaster, they made an inauspicious beginning for the new reign.

HARMONY OR DISCORD?

The 'senseless dreams' speech suggests that Nicholas II had quickly come to see the zemstvos as antithetical to the Imperial regime. Pobedonostsev's advice would only have reinforced this view; what he disliked most about the zemstvos was that any expansion of their activities at the local level would negatively affect his plans for the rejuvenation of the parish life of the Orthodox Church. When a government commission set up in the wake of the 1891 famine to examine the problem of poor relief recommended that its administration be secularized and placed in the hands of the zemstvos, Pobedonostsev sent the Ministry of the Interior a tirade that attacked every aspect of the plan, accusing the zemstvos of having imposed on a defenceless peasantry new tax burdens and a new layer of irresponsible officials [59]. On this issue Witte was, for once, on the same side as the procurator, not only because any strengthening of local autonomy would obstruct his plans for state-directed economic development, but also because he believed, with good reason, that the provincial gentry who dominated most zemstvo assemblies were bent on protecting their own agrarian interests, and would tax commerce and industry far more heavily than landed property [65, 114]. When, at the end of the decade, a plan was advanced to extend zemstvo institutions to the western and southwestern provinces, Witte wrote for the emperor a lengthy memorandum in which he claimed that zemstvos were self-aggrandizing elected institutions which were fundamentally hostile to, and irreconcilable with, the autocratic regime [*Doc. 5*]. Nicholas found this argument so persuasive that he dismissed the minister who had sponsored the project. It is no coincidence that the same argument about irreconcilability was being made within a year or two by the so-called zemstvo opposition, whose leaders were ready to join forces with the revolutionaries in a tactical alliance that sought to wrest major political concessions from the Imperial regime.

Were the zemstvos bound to clash with the tsarist regime? At moments of discord, such claims were made on both sides, but archival research has shown that conflicts were the exception rather than the rule, and that for much of their history the zemstvos functioned in harmony with the bureaucracy, so much so that the Senate, the final court of appeal against an arbitrary administration, sometimes received complaints about zemstvos for their capricious, abusive, and vengeful behaviour [34]. The idea that the zemstvos, simply because they were elected, embodied the democratic will is ludicrous; the electoral law gave disproportionate weight to gentry landowners before 1890 through high property qualifications, and after 1890 by means of quotas based on legal estate (soslovie) membership. Peasants, well aware of these limitations on their participation and especially of the extra tax burden that they were now forced to shoulder, regarded zemstvos as at best an expensive luxury, and at worst as yet another creation of 'the bosses' (*nachalstvo* *) [18].

The conflict that developed at the turn of the century between centralizers in the Ministry of the Interior and advocates of zemstvo autonomy was not the culmination of some inevitable tension between elected bodies and appointed bureaucrats; it happened chiefly because the central government began to concern itself quite seriously with matters of local government. Despite official claim that the zemstvos needed to be restrained from interfering in matters of national or Imperial concern, it was, ironically, the reverse process that was at work: ministries in St Petersburg were becoming more involved in local zemstvo affairs, and doing so more regularly. This dramatic change of course was spurred first by the huge increase in zemstvo activities, budgets, and taxes during the 1890s, a situation which naturally led to competition for scarce tax revenues between the various levels of government; and secondly by the prolific increase in the number of zemstvo employees – agronomists, statisticians, teachers and medical personnel – many of whom, the security agencies were convinced, were revolutionaries using these positions as a cover for their subversive activities among the peasantry. In fact, most of these zemstvo employees, although certainly reform-minded, were on the whole more committed to professional than political goals [37, 55]. Such subtleties eluded the police mentality that was shared by successive ministers of the interior.

RADICALISM REJUVENATED

The famine, greeted on the left as conclusive evidence of the regime's incompetence, acted as a catalyst for the renewal of revolutionary activity, the latter largely in limbo since the suppression of terrorism after 1881. The regime's efforts to provide relief and stimulate charitable assistance brought it nothing but contempt from those horrified by such a flagrant demonstration of social injustice. To be sure, almost all educated Russians found the famine and epidemics disconcerting reminders of Russian backwardness; civilized countries, they assured one another, did not suffer from famines, nor were they so prone to the ravages of epidemic disease. The moderates' response was a strong reaffirmation of the importance of popular education and public health, but the radicals went much further. For them, these events were less a national embarrassment than an indictment of the tsarist regime, which in their minds already stood convicted of moral responsibility for the misery and exploitation experienced by the vast mass of the people. That these sufferings appeared to flow directly from the government's economic policies naturally outraged those raised in the intellectual milieu of Russian populism, and opened up for debate the broader question of how radicals ought to respond to the changes that capitalist industrial development was bringing to Russian society. In this new phase of the long-standing debate over Russia's relationship with Western Europe, Marxism would play a more important role than populism [80, 117].

How could Marxism have been thought relevant to an overwhelmingly agricultural country where, as late as 1900, factory and railroad workers and miners together totalled a mere 2 per cent of the population, a few tiny proletarian islands in a vast peasant sea? For one thing, it was not the immediate but the potential size of the proletariat (or the bourgeoisie) that mattered, and thanks to the regime's enthusiasm for industrial development, the rapid growth of both capitalist employers and an industrial labour force seemed assured. Another reason for Marxism's appeal to Russian intellectuals and would-be revolutionaries was the quasi-scientific certainty upon which its analysis of social development was believed to rest. Confronted by a regime that included antimodernists such as Pobedonostsev, and that routinely kept order by employing the army, the police, the censorship, and a host of administrative restrictions, it was extremely difficult to remain optimistic about the prospects for revolution; yet Marxism offered just such missing certainties – that revolution was inevitable, and was sure to produce a more just society.

These assurances were especially welcome during the 1890s because there was otherwise little cause for optimism. The peasantry's largely fatalistic response to the misery of 1891–92 had done nothing to justify the populists' faith in their revolutionary capacities; on the contrary, the 'cholera riots' seemed to demonstrate that ignorance and senseless violence were deeply embedded in the peasant mentality. Witte's headlong rush to industrialize the country, on the other hand, seemed likely to reverse traditions of tsarist paternalism, thereby giving employers a free hand to exploit their workers to the limits of human endurance. Yet on this issue Marxism offered an additional assurance: no government, perhaps least of all the tsarist regime, would be able successfully to control the social changes that industrialization would bring. Thanks to the workings of Marx's dialectic, once the path of industrialization was chosen, it would lead inexorably to proletarian revolution and the building of socialism. Instead of anguishing about the spectre of a capitalist future, as the populists were wont to do, Marxists could grit their teeth and welcome the incipient bourgeois revolution as a necessary, indeed a vital, step on the road to socialism.

Marxism offered Russians a road map to the future, but no clearly visible arrow saying 'you are here'. Predictably, the early converts agonized, argued and quarrelled over where to place the crucial arrow. Did the obvious lag between Russian and European social development mean that Russians would be little more than spectators while their more advanced neighbours proceeded through the proletarian revolution to the building of socialism? Or alternatively, as Marx himself hinted, might this time lag work to Russia's benefit, enabling it to bypass the bourgeois stage of social development and thus proceed more quickly to the socialist future? Was it perhaps conceivable that the uniqueness of their own social and economic development could enable Russians to bring the revolution to Europe, rather than vice versa? The answers to these tantalizing questions logically determined both the nature and the time frame of revolution in Russia, and hence the appropriate role and tasks of any Marxist organization, especially its relationship to other political groupings, and to workers' organizations and movements of social protest. For Marxists, finding the right answer to the 'Where is here?' question was complicated by the fact that although the map was fixed, the social terrain itself was constantly shifting; making the appropriate adaptations to circumstance was often more a matter of personality and temperament than of ideology. Genuinely different answers emerged, but because the adherents of each believed theirs to be *the* truly scientific interpretation, disputes quickly began to resemble religious conflicts between orthodox and heretical beliefs.

Although the founder of Russian Marxism, George Plekhanov, conceded that Russian backwardness could have some small effect on the process, he firmly believed that socialist revolution would occur there only after it had happened in Europe, and that Russia was bound to experience both a bourgeois and a proletarian revolution. According to him, the backwardness of Russian workers impelled Marxist intellectuals to form a party that would define workers' interests not merely as higher wages and shorter hours but as including the broader revolutionary struggle for the achievement of socialism. Peter Struve disagreed, arguing that it might take decades, perhaps even centuries, for capitalist exploitation to bring workers to the revolutionary boil, and therefore there was no immediate need for Marxists to risk their future by engaging in illegal revolutionary activity. This sounded too much like the German revisionist Eduard Bernstein, and Struve was soon no longer welcome in the Marxist camp. When another group advocated that economic, not political, goals ought to take first priority, they were labelled 'economists', and cast out of the fold. While these arguments raged, the textile workers of St Petersburg successfully set their own radical pace, striking in 1896–97 for a reduction of the working day from thirteen to ten and a half hours. Vladimir Lenin and Julius Martov were members of the Social Democratic groups that merged in October, 1895 to form the St. Petersburg Union of Struggle for the Emancipation of the Working Class, but both men were almost immediately arrested and the subsequent influence of this organization on the striking workers is problematic [83]. Within two years, radical workers were publishing their own journals, cautioning their readers about intellectuals who 'by some sad (or laughable) misunderstanding regard themselves as born revolutionaries ... It is well to remember that today's revolutionaries are tomorrow's prosecutors, judges, engineers, factory inspectors ...' [94 p. 146]. Needless to say, such striking evidence of the maturity of worker-activists did not provoke the Marxists to rethink the need for a party of intellectuals to guide the course of the coming revolution.

3 THE DAWN OF THE NEW CENTURY, 1899–1904

INDUSTRY AND LABOUR

Russia entered a period of uncertainty when the depression of 1900 brought the industrial boom to an end. It was signalled by a slump in 1899, as foreign investors, jittery about war in South Africa and disturbances in the Far East, reassessed the altered international situation. As the share of foreign capital investment directed to Russia slowed to a trickle, two spectacular business failures and numerous bankruptcies raised the stakes, helping to turn the slump into a depression from which the country seemed unable to recover. Industrial prices fell rapidly, and output – especially in heavy industry – shrank as a result. Strikes, rising unemployment, and a sharp fall in profits were the inevitable consequences. Witte's critics, seemingly invigorated by the prospect of disaster, renewed their complaints against his policies: not only were they turning Russia into an economic colony of Western Europe, but also this depression now demonstrated how few benefits and how much real hardship could result from that inferior status. In fact, the critics laid too much blame on foreigners: their own government helped to cause the depression. Faced with declining tax revenues from agriculture, it was placing fewer orders in the heavy industrial sector; its sudden change of heart, attributable in part to the near completion of a number of large projects including the Trans-Siberian line, was dramatically symbolized by a 10 per cent drop in railway-related orders in 1900. For the next several years, industrialists responded to the continuing depression by forming cartels and other associations to regulate production and sales, especially for steel, fossil fuels, base metals, and metallurgical enterprises. They felt impelled to look to their own interests in part because Witte's position and influence in economic affairs were much less certain after 1899 than before, even though he retained the position of Minister of Finance until 1903.

Some of Witte's critics believed that paternalistic concern for the welfare of all the tsar's subjects should guide the regime's policies towards industry and labour. This was not a new idea: in the 1880s factory legislation had attempted to limit the exploitation of workers by establishing rules for the fair and timely payment of wages, by restricting the employment of women and children, and by giving the factory inspectors a wider jurisdiction over employment practices and conditions. Supporters of paternalism knew what extensive disorders had been caused in Europe by small but unruly groups of industrial workers during the revolutions of 1848 and during the Paris Commune uprising in 1871. To prevent a repetition of these events in Russia, they believed the government should ensure that employers treated their workers fairly, so that the latter would have no reason to form unions or foment disturbances. Needless to say, Witte did not share these views; his inclination was to remove as many restrictions on employment practices as possible. He might have preferred to eliminate the factory inspectors altogether, but after the textile workers' strikes in St Petersburg, he settled for turning them into spies and informers, which was at least preferable to their acting as advocates for the interests of workers. These events, coupled with police discoveries that underground Marxist groups were attempting to establish links with activist workers, forced senior officials in the Ministry of the Interior to reconsider a long-standing institutional myth which held that the loyalty and deference of Russian workers could be relied on, provided they were treated fairly, because so many of them retained ties with their villages. Perhaps Russian workers were not inoculated against socialism after all, they conceded; perhaps their earlier complacency had been ill-advised.

With Witte knocked off balance by the industrial slump, advocates of paternalism in Moscow seized the moment to foster a new initiative aimed at beating the socialists at their own game. Instead of trying to render unions and strikes unnecessary, the paternalists now argued that since they were already facts of life, the wisest course was to co-opt them for the purposes of the regime. The specifics of this approach originated in a plan drawn up in 1898 by the Chief of the Secret Police in Moscow, Sergei Zubatov [67, 98]. Naive and imaginative but not stupid, Zubatov believed that with careful nurturing, Russian workers would blossom as loyal and devoted supporters of the monarchy. All that was necessary, he argued, was that the regime be courageous enough to intervene in the labour market before the greed and indifference of employers drove their frustrated workers into the arms of the socialists. Zubatov wanted workers to be given all the associations they wanted, not only trade unions but also educational and self-help organizations, all run by workers themselves but – and this was the crucial point – supervised and partially funded by the police. It was absolutely essential to the success of the scheme that these unions be, and be seen to be, militant and effective; if this meant discreet arm-twisting to ensure the co-operation of employers, then so be it. Zubatov's proposal, couched in language suggesting that the greediest bosses were Jews, was well received not only by his superior General Trepov, the city's Chief of Police, but also by Nicholas II's uncle, Grand Duke Sergei, who as Governor-General of Moscow was the tsar's personal representative in the city.

In St Petersburg the response was mixed. Paternalists in the Ministry of the Interior, while agreeing with the principle of state intervention, thought this particular scheme hare-brained, even hazardous; it might easily backfire, driving the workers irretrievably towards radicalism. Witte, who only learned what was afoot when an employer complained of police harassment, furiously attacked the dangerous amateurism of its promoters, and called for an immediate stop to this absurd experiment in police socialism. He could make no headway, however, against the zealous Minister of the Interior, Dmitrii Sipiagin, largely because the antisemitism and naive popular monarchism of Zubatov's scheme had now attracted the tsar himself [60]. Zubatov delighted his royal patrons by putting 50,000 workers on the streets for a loyal demonstration to mark the fortieth anniversary of the liberation of the serfs in February, 1902. A year later, however, another Zubatov enterprise went disastrously awry, implicating him in fomenting a general strike in Odessa; Plehve was now Minister of the Interior – Sipiagin having been assassinated – and he had no choice but to dismiss the now discredited Zubatov. The idea of cultivating a loyalist working class was almost, but not quite, destroyed; it would soon surface again under the charismatic leadership of a priest, Father Gapon.

RUSSIFICATION

The tsar found demonstrations of popular monarchism attractive because they gave him hope that loyal workers as well as peasants could be deployed against the various forces of subversion and corruption: unruly students, socialist agitators, know-it-all professionals, and 'Jewish' employers. These sentiments were fully shared by Plehve, who made no secret of his anti-semitism [*Doc. 6*]. From their point of view, only if the Russian heartland were politically reliable could the empire deal with serious threats to its integrity, especially those posed by the non-Russian minorities in the borderlands. This was, after all, the *Russian* Empire: it might contain many different ethnic groups, but Russian national identity was the only one officially recognized. Russian monarchists thought that the Habsburgs had been foolish to accommodate the Hungarians by turning their empire into a Dual Monarchy. They were determined to resist any similar move towards federalism in Russia, and their intransigent support for the autocracy was based on the not unrealistic belief that without it the empire would disintegrate.

By far the strongest claims for a separate national identity came from the Poles, whose venerable kingdom, as they persisted in reminding the Russians, had been part of Christendom long before anyone had heard of Moscow. After the 1863 rebellion proved their 'disloyalty', Alexander II's government set out deliberately to integrate them into the empire by destroying every vestige of Polish national and cultural identity. The separate Polish viceroyalty was eliminated, and the 'Vistula provinces', as Russian Poland was now called, were run by governors appointed in St. Petersburg. Poles were forced to learn Russian in school, and were required to speak Russian for transacting all official business, including judicial proceedings. In the hope of weakening the Poles' attachment to the Roman Catholic Church, the Russians confiscated its property, diverting it to secular purposes; with a conqueror's arrogance, they also built a large Orthodox cathedral in central Warsaw. Polish Uniates were forcibly converted to Orthodoxy. The predictable result of all these measures was to heap new hatreds and resentments on top of an already profound national humiliation; the Poles' grudging submission to Russian authority was maintained partly by the presence of a large garrison that was really an army of occupation, and partly by the desperate hope of some patriots that if liberalism triumphed in Russia, then Polish independence would be restored.

The treatment of Poland provided a model for the Russification of other borderland areas, a policy supported by both Alexander III and Nicholas II. There were several other varieties of conservative nationalism in nineteenth-century Russia, but the officially-sanctioned uniformity embodied in the idea of Russification drew support not only from the ruling dynasty, but also from security-conscious army officers and from a Church hierarchy keen on attracting converts. For the bureaucrats of the day, who were better educated, more professional, and less tied to the land than their gentry forbears, Russification had some appeal because it offered the hope of a more homogeneous, and therefore presumably less unruly, population [100]. Pobedonostsev was far too intelligent not to realize that crude measures alone would be counterproductive; ingeniously, he tried to forge a transcending 'all-Russian', imperial identity that would appear less oppressive, but this was too transparent a fraud to be taken seriously outside a small circle of devotees [28, 110]. Russification, even in its crudest form, was an impossible goal because the regime lacked the manpower, efficiency, and systematic approach that such a programme would have required; in any case, the borderlands were far too disparate for a 'one-size-fits-all' solution.

That Russifying the borderlands was beyond the capacities of the regime did not deter supporters from the idea of attempting the impossible, with results that ranged from unfortunate to disastrous. In the case of the Ukraine, which had benefited enormously from the economic boom of the 1890s, the Russians overreacted to demands for cultural autonomy first expressed by intellectuals who lacked significant popular support, thereby virtually ensuring the rapid growth of a Ukrainian nationalist underground, albeit with Austrian connivance. In the Baltic provinces, the German landowning elite had given loyal service to the Russian Empire for decades, while the incipient nationalist movements among the largely peasant Latvians and Estonians were directed primarily against their German overlords. Yet in the 1880s, a series of heavy-handed measures directed against both Protestantism and the German language turned many Baltic Germans against Russia; they also taught Latvian and Estonian nationalists the futility of expecting the Russians to dispossess landowners – German or not – in favour of landless peasants. In the south, ostensibly to avoid conflict with the Ottoman Empire, the Russians suddenly turned against their erstwhile friends, the Armenians, who naturally resisted a Russian assault on the schools run by their national (Gregorian Christian) Church. In retaliation, the Russians encouraged Muslims from the neighbouring Azerbaijan region to attack the Armenians. Thus, from the Baltic to the Caucasus, programmes of Russification awakened the dormant and the indifferent, turned moderates into radicals, and friends into foes; only fools measured their success by counting the number of closed churches, forced conversions to Russian Orthodoxy, and classrooms full of bitter and resentful students.

The Grand Duchy of Finland was a special case: its fully autonomous status derived from the 1809 agreement that transferred it from the Swedish to the Russian Empire. So long as the Russians honoured the rights and privileges of Finnish autonomy, the Finns had no grounds for complaint, let alone rebellion or revolution; indeed the cultural nationalists in the Ukraine would have been delighted to enjoy even a tiny fraction of Finnish liberties. For their part, most Finns understandably wished only to retain their liberties intact, and to do so indefinitely. By the end of the nineteenth century, however, the Russian government, with an eye on the growing strength of Germany, sought from the Grand Duchy a larger contribution to Imperial defence than the traditional arrangements required. Defence quickly became the main, although not the sole, issue: Finland's growing industrial economy threatened to compete with Russia's, while its independent jurisdiction continually frustrated Russian policemen who were well aware that known revolutionaries crossed the border whenever it suited them. A dispute in 1899 over the amount and extent of military service by Finnish conscripts escalated into a larger crisis when Nicholas II issued a manifesto which asserted that in matters of Imperial interest, the laws of the empire would take precedence within the Grand Duchy over laws made by its own Diet and Senate. The manifesto was partially the work of Plehve, who was then State Secretary for Finland in St Petersburg; its timing – published while the Finnish Diet was preparing to consider the most recent Russian demands – was regarded as a further provocation. Half a million signatures were speedily collected for a petition to the tsar/grand duke, demanding the redress of grievances, but instead of preserving Finland's rights and privileges as his predecessors had done, Nicholas stood by while his Governor-General, Bobrikov, dismantled them one after another. Bobrikov believed that Russia had never completed its conquest of Finland, and sought to repair the mistake [*Doc. 7*]. In 1900, Russian was made the official language of public administration; Bobrikov countered Finnish resistance by staffing senior positions with Russians brought from St Petersburg. When Finns refused to comply with a new (1901) conscription law that virtually abolished their autonomous army, Bobrikov replied by suspending what was left of the 1809 constitution. Most Finns were appalled but not surprised when he was assassinated by a young radical in June, 1904. In the following year, and for several years thereafter, the Russian government would reap the whirlwind that it had sown in the Grand Duchy [111].

PEASANT UNREST

In 1902, disturbances broke out in two southern provinces (Poltava and Kharkov) and in the lower Volga region; peasants took out their frustrations on the persons and property of local landlords. Traditional explanations for these events have emphasized that the perennial problems of productivity and overpopulation were exacerbated by the difficulties most peasants faced in meeting the redemption dues owed to a government that was already relying heavily on revenues from indirect taxes imposed on basic consumer items such as kerosene, matches, sugar, tea and vodka. In these circumstances, so the argument runs, many found themselves trapped in a morass of debt and deprivation, first borrowing at high interest to meet tax payments, then scrambling to keep up the interest payments, then facing punishments – whipping, confiscation of land, perhaps exile – when they were unable to avoid defaulting on those payments. Such explanations have not gone unchallenged: in an alternative interpretation, peasants fell into arrears because they chose not to make those payments, preferring instead to save their money, or to purchase consumer goods (hence explaining why sales tax revenues increased); even received wisdom concerning levels of food production and the nutritional inadequacy of peasant diet have been called into question [48, 103]. On these controversial issues, including the local peculiarities that explain why unrest was confined to certain regions, there is still considerable disagreement.

In any case, contemporary opponents of government policy, whether populists or paternalists, were far more interested in the general than the particular significance of the disturbances. Their attention focused on two main issues: the extent to which the unrest proved that critics of the regime's fiscal policies were correct; and the possibility – exciting or alarming, depending on one's point of view – that the peasants were at last becoming a potentially revolutionary force. The ensuing debates were by no means confined to bureaucrats and publicists of various stripes: provincial landowners had always been handy targets of peasant resentment, and therefore they were also concerned, usually in a very immediate way, about whether the government could prevent further disturbances. Their often narrow approach was balanced by the self-consciously grander aspirations of the students attending Russia's universities and technical institutes, most of whom easily conflated freeing themselves from administrative tutelage with liberating the common people from an oppressive regime.

In government circles, the 1902 disturbances strengthened the convictions of those, like Witte, who had come to believe that only the abolition of the commune and the encouragement of individual peasant landholding would solve the problems of rural Russia. Almost as if he anticipated the unrest, Witte had earlier in the year appealed to the tsar to focus the country's attention on this great task by taking personal direction of it, as his grandfather Alexander II had done in planning the emancipation of the serfs. Nicholas was far more cautious, and was afraid to destroy such a venerable Russian institution as the commune, especially when conservatives insisted that its alleged economic deficiencies were less important than its stabilizing role in the countryside. Senior officials in his Ministry of the Interior advised that its abolition would certainly lead to a period of instability that might prove even more dangerous than the unrest already evident. Yet although the tsar rejected Witte's appeal, he nevertheless made the finance minister chairman of a newly-created Special Commission on the Needs of the Agricultural Industry, a move that some interpreted to mean that Nicholas had reluctantly accepted the need for sweeping change in rural Russia. That this was a false hope soon became apparent: the tsar refused to stipulate that the traditional jurisdiction of the Ministry of the Interior over peasant affairs should now be subordinated to Witte's interdepartmental Commission, in effect giving the defenders of the commune at least as strong an institutional base as that of the would-be abolitionists. Although Witte attempted to draw support from beyond St Petersburg by proposing that the Commission consult with local committees in the provinces, he faced even more formidable opposition when Plehve replaced Sipiagin as Minister of the Interior. Although Witte retained the chairmanship of the Special Commission after he lost the Finance Ministry in 1903, he was by then in no position to bully the tsar into abolishing the commune. After Plehve himself was assassinated by a terrorist's bomb in 1904, Nicholas was even less likely to contemplate measures that might cause further instability.

Not surprisingly, the peasant disturbances evoked an entirely different response from the populist wing of the intelligentsia, which was rejuvenated by this apparent evidence that the revolutionary potential of the peasantry was still very much alive. What ensued was much more than a revival of the naive populism of the 1870s: Victor Chernov, who emerged as the most important leader of the Socialist Revolutionary (SR) Party, formed in 1902, readily acknowledged that in a Russia transformed by capitalist industry, there was much to be learned from the writings of Marx and Engels. In his hands, agrarian socialism adapted both its theoretical basis and its practical activity to the changing economic and social conditions of Russia's industrial revolution. Abandoning the earlier idea of an exclusively peasant revolution that would lead directly to the creation of socialism, the SRs now integrated the Marxian conception of necessary historical stages, and revised their conception of eventual socialist revolution to include leading roles for both peasants and industrial workers. Where an earlier generation of populists had wrung their hands in despair over the coming of capitalism, the SRs were now able to appreciate its revolutionary potential, and therefore were able to respond more positively to this phase of economic development, although Chernov still hoped to preserve from its destructive inroads both the village community and the uniquely Russian characteristics of peasant socialism. In this new garb, the SRs were active propagandists and organizers not only in the countryside, where many village schoolteachers were party members or sympathizers, but also among factory workers in St. Petersburg and elsewhere [78, 88]. Their message of a revolution made jointly by peasants and workers struck a responsive chord among the latter, and the old idea that the SRs were simply the voice of peasant Russia was no longer tenable. On the shop floor, as well as among dispossessed agricultural labourers, they were rivals of, and competitors with, the explicitly Marxist Social Democrats [72]. Nevertheless, the extremism of earlier revolutionary populism still survived in the SRs' 'Fighting Organization', an underground terrorist group responsible for several noteworthy assassinations, including those of two successive Ministers of the Interior (Sipiagin and Plehve). For some impatient revolutionary temperaments, propaganda by the deed was more immediately satisfying than its less dramatic forms.

BOLSHEVIKS AND MENSHEVIKS

The Social Democrats stood somewhat apart from these events because they were preoccupied with intra-party struggles over doctrine and organization. The debate continued to focus on finding the organization and tactics appropriate to the stage of development reached by Russia's working class. However, instead of attacking dissenters against party orthodoxy, the party soon split into two seemingly irreconcilable factions that expended at least as much energy battling each other as they did on combating the enemies of the proletariat. In these clashes individual personalities undoubtedly played a significant role, one that many observers (and some of the participants) considered ironic, given the importance that Marx and Plekhanov had attached to impersonal forces in historical development.

By 1900, Lenin and Martov had returned from political exile, and both were working with Plekhanov, Paul Axelrod and other leading Marxists on the editorial board of the newly founded party journal

Iskra (The Spark). However, while this group were zealously defending party orthodoxy against revisionists and 'economists', Lenin was quietly formulating a Marxist variant of his own, one which found expression in his 1902 pamphlet, *What Is to Be Done?* In his view, Marxists were too optimistic about the revolutionary potential of the working class; workers themselves would never go beyond what he contemptuously termed a trade-union consciousness, and hence Social Democrats ought to keep them at a distance so that they would neither corrupt nor dilute the purity and single-mindedness of the party's revolutionary struggle. The kind of small, conspiratorial party of professional revolutionaries that Lenin sought 'implied nothing less than the permanent tutelage of the proletariat by the radical intelligentsia'. [16 *p. 38*]. Why his views did not provoke an immediate row is unclear, but their implications became all too plain when questions of organization and tactics were discussed at a party congress held in Brussels and (thanks to disruption by the Belgian police) London in the summer of 1903. Although the intended purpose of the congress was to bring together numerous Marxist factions – some of them Russian, some Polish, some Jewish – into one unified Russian Social Democratic Workers' Party, Lenin took every opportunity to expound his views and to muster support for his position on crucial votes. Although Martov and his supporters managed to stave off defeat on the issue of the definition of party membership, Lenin manoeuvred his way to victory on several other important votes. Sensing the advantage to be derived from bold distortion, he immediately began to call his supporters 'Bolsheviks' and Martov's followers 'Mensheviks', from the Russian words for majority and minority. In the wake of the congress Lenin began to devote more attention to the peasantry, whose recently displayed revolutionary potential made them possible allies of the workers, and to the possibility of using them in an armed uprising against the regime that was planned and co-ordinated, naturally, by professional revolutionaries who shared his views. Martov and Plekhanov continued to believe in the gradualist approach of a broadly-based party of workers and intellectuals, and worried that Lenin was risking disaster for Russian social democracy by trying to do too much, too soon. Axelrod, meanwhile, warned that a successful Bolshevik uprising would simply replace the despotism of Nicholas II with that of Lenin. At the time, he simply meant to alert Social Democrats to the dangers inherent in Lenin's approach, but in 1918 many would see his warning as a prediction that was striking in its accuracy.

THE LIBERATION MOVEMENT

The recurring nightmare of Russian monarchists was an alliance between moderate and radical opponents of the regime, and this finally became a reality in 1903. During an earlier crisis at the end of the 1870s, moderate reformers in the zemstvos had been outraged when the government seemed to ignore the huge gulf that separated them from revolutionary terrorists [120]. A quarter of a century later, that gulf had narrowed considerably, even if more liberals than revolutionaries were ready to recognize the fact and behave accordingly.

The growing influence of the empire's new professionals was at least partially responsible for this great change. Although still numerically small, Russian academics, lawyers, physicians, and engineers formed groups whose increasing coherence and assertiveness provided a congenial environment for the development of new ideas about the organization of civil society, perhaps in the long run a more congenial environment than the zemstvos, despite the undeniably important contributions of a vocal minority of gentry landowners who espoused the cause of zemstvo liberalism. The latter had come to equate liberalism with freedom from bureaucratic control, and hence they sought to strengthen the autonomy, budgetary powers, and jurisdiction of the zemstvos, although they were often noticeably reluctant to pass these greater powers on to the professionals whom they employed. For their part, the professionals were motivated principally by a shared respect for the power of reason, the authority of knowledge, and the claims of expertise. All too often, in their view, the social and political structure of the Russian Empire put those lacking expert knowledge in positions of authority, while those who possessed that knowledge found themselves in subordinate positions where their advice was either ignored or not even sought. Although some version of this conflict was common to most countries in an age of growing sophistication in matters of public administration, in Russia it sometimes seemed that the obstacles to professionalization, and to increasing the influence of professionals in society, were so entrenched and so formidable that only an extensive remaking of the existing order would eliminate them [19]. Only a minority of Russian professionals consistently put general political issues ahead of particular professional concerns, but those who reached this degree of frustration usually found themselves on the left wing of the political spectrum.

Another important component of the new political climate was the fact that some members of the intelligentsia were prepared to put aside, at least for the moment, the narrow sectarianism that had so far prevented any coalescing of opposition forces. Both a herald and an agent of this change in outlook was the founding in 1902 of a new opposition journal, *Osvobozhdenie (Liberation)*, edited in Stuttgart (and later Paris) by the former Marxist theoretician Struve, and smuggled back to Russia via the underground [*Doc. 8*]. Disillusioned by the intolerance and infighting of the Marxists, Struve decided, with strong support from leading zemstvo liberals, to attempt the creation of a broad opposition front. His novel message, startling in its lack of dogmatism, was that revolutionaries and liberals 'in essence move in the same direction and merely go to different terminal points' [36 *p.86*]; if this were true, then both groups could work together to bring down the autocracy. Except for the Social Democrats, who seemed temperamentally incapable of minimizing differences of any kind, the response to Struve's new tactic was extraordinarily positive; groups of self-styled 'Liberationists' began to meet throughout 1903 in several Russian locations. In January, 1904, a more formal organization, the Union of Liberation, was created in St Petersburg to pursue a definite political programme that gave first priority to the establishment of constitutional government and the introduction of basic civil liberties for all [*Doc. 9*]. Local branches of the Union began to attract support not only from left-wing liberals in the zemstvos and from professionals, but also from non-Marxist revolutionaries, many of them SRs.

The most outspoken radical among the Liberationists was Paul Miliukov, who had begun his career as a history professor at the University of Moscow and was well known in academic circles for incisive lectures and a definitive published study of the peasantry in eighteenth-century Russia. Like Struve, Miliukov was an urban intellectual, but where the former was a disillusioned Marxist, the latter was an enthusiastic positivist with a wholehearted and utterly uncritical faith in the virtues of constitutional government. Because of his intense admiration for Western political culture, particularly the British parliamentary system, Miliukov's biographer has called him 'a Russian European' [90], while an English contemporary thought of him as a Liberal in the tradition of Gladstone [75]. He knew enough constitutional history to appreciate that in the seventeenth century, it had been necessary for Englishmen to defend the rights of parliament by taking up arms against an intransigent monarch, and that knowledge gave him the assurance that if Russians could join together in opposition to the autocracy, then the cause of constitutional government was certain to triumph. Achieving this goal was so important to him that he was prepared to join forces with any group or individual prepared to make common cause against the tsarist regime, and to overlook for the moment what might in the long run prove to be sub-

stantial ideological differences. The willingness of Struve and Miliukov to co-operate with revolutionaries, while supported by some,
made other liberals uneasy, partly because they disliked violence and
feared its consequences, and partly because they were not wholly convinced that their country would be better off under a parliamentary
regime. The latter group believed that the tsarist regime might still be
persuaded that the rule of law was the most necessary of all reforms
in a country where those who governed had yet to observe it.

As the Liberationists moved to the left, moderate liberals in the
zemstvos found an articulate and morally compelling spokesman in
Dmitrii Shipov, president of the executive board of the Moscow provincial zemstvo. Shipov belonged to that group whose deferential plea
for a greater zemstvo voice in national affairs had been spurned by
Nicholas II in his 'senseless dreams' speech; because national zemstvo
conferences were forbidden, he and other zemstvo deputies had met
informally since then to discuss the political situation and to promote
their cause. In Shipov's cautious liberalism there were strong elements
of romantic nationalism: where Miliukov looked to the English Civil
War, Shipov looked to Russian tradition, above all to that Muscovite
institution called the assembly of the land (*zemskii sobor**) which had
played a significant role in the government of Russia in the sixteenth
and early seventeenth centuries. In his view, the true Russian political
tradition was one of a benevolent monarch ruling in accordance with
law, and desiring to be guided by the loyal and humble advice of representatives of the nation. To impose legal restrictions on the powers
of a tsar was in Shipov's view unthinkable, but by the same token it
was entirely conceivable that a truly benevolent tsar would recognize
the need for *de facto* limitations and adopt them voluntarily. Harmony, not divisiveness, was at the heart of Shipov's fundamentally
antipolitical conception of government: what he abhorred most about
Western parliamentarism was its encouragement of factionalism and
partisanship. The zemstvos, he believed, embodied a truly harmonious and therefore uniquely Russian approach to self-government;
hence the urgency of his desire that Nicholas II create a national zemstvo body that would, in the best Russian tradition, help him to
govern the empire. Shipov's position was initially far more acceptable
to the vast majority of zemstvo deputies than the more radical programme of the Union of Liberation, but its credibility depended on
evidence that the tsar was likely to move in this direction of his own
accord, and Nicholas II gave no such sign. Indeed, the behaviour of
the regime simply undercut the position of moderates like Shipov and
strengthened the appeal of the Liberationists' programme. To make

matters worse, the Russian government became embroiled in a series of disputes with Japan, blundering into a war that seemed to demonstrate the incompetence of the tsarist regime and to bolster the claims of its severest critics.

4 RUSSIA IN TURMOIL, 1904–1906

EASTERN ADVENTURES

By 1900, the Chinese Empire was faltering, but so many countries were interested in its fate that a partition agreement was out of the question. Not only Russia and Japan, the nearest neighbours, but also Britain, France, Germany, and the United States had a stake in the imperialist competition in the Far East. Unlike the Western powers, who chose to locate their trade concessions and coastal enclaves from the Yellow Sea southwards, Russia and Japan had designs on Manchuria itself, and on Korea and the adjacent Liaotung Peninsula. In other circumstances, these two rivals conceivably might have reached a durable spheres-of-interest agreement that assigned Manchuria to Russia and Korea to Japan. Instead, Japan was provoked by Russia's behaviour – by turns inexplicable, duplicitous, and menacing – to an act of war that put the two countries into open conflict for twenty months, with profound consequences that were felt especially in far off St Petersburg.

Russia wanted northern Manchuria not only as a base from which to open up the commercial markets of the Far East, but also because it offered a potential short cut to Vladivostok, reducing the journey by more than a thousand miles, over a route that was relatively inexpensive to construct. Icebound during the winter months, Vladivostok was scarcely a sailor's dream, so the Russian navy dreamed of better alternatives: possibly the Korean port of Inchon, or Port Arthur at the tip of the Liaotung Peninsula. The Japanese, for their part, wanted Korea not only to keep out the Russians, but also to secure complete control over the Straits of Tsushima. When the Japanese easily defeated China in 1895 – a campaign likely accelerated by Russia's decision to build the Trans-Siberian line – they exacted both an indemnity and territorial concessions, including southern Manchuria and the naval base at Port Arthur. The Russians, who had been outraged when diplomatic action deprived them of the spoils of victory in an earlier war against the Ottoman Empire, now proceeded to give the Japanese a dose of the same medicine. With the agreement of Germany and France, and useful help from French bankers, the Russians engineered a diplomatic *coup* whereby Japan was forced to accept a larger indemnity in return for not disrupting the territorial *status quo*. For the grateful Chinese, the lesser evil was to give Russia the railway concession that it sought in order to build the Chinese Eastern Railway across Manchuria to Vladivostok. The Russians had clearly won this round.

In 1897–98, China was again pressured by the great powers, with Germany, Britain, and Russia all watching carefully lest one succeed in outdoing the others. After much agonizing – none of it over moral issues – the Russians extracted a lease that gave them control of Port Arthur and the Liaotung Peninsula; after the other powers made compensatory gains of their own, the Japanese understandably thought that they had been deceived as well as outmanoeuvred. When a wave of anti-foreign sentiment in China culminated in the Boxer Rebellion of 1900, the Russians used the occasion to dispatch troops to Manchuria, ostensibly to protect the railway, but also to establish a bargaining position: their troops would be withdrawn when China granted Russia what was in effect exclusive control of trade and commerce, not only in Manchuria, but in other border areas such as Mongolia and Sinkiang. At this point the Russians overplayed their hand; all the other powers were now against them, Britain and Japan formalizing their mutual and profound distrust of Russian intentions in a treaty of alliance, signed early in 1902, which recognized Japan's 'special interest' in Korea.

At this point, fatefully, Nicholas II decided to take a larger personal role in determining Russian policy in the Far East. He himself firmly believed that Russia's future lay in Asia, and openly sympathized with the navy's desire for a warm-water port on the Pacific, but for more than five years he had felt pushed this way and that by frequently conflicting advice from his ministers of finance, foreign affairs, and war. Frustrated that officials and bureaucrats kept getting in the way, Nicholas was easily persuaded to put his own, more forceful, stamp on events by a group of Russian aristocrats whose influence at Court enabled them to bypass the ministers. This group, incorporated as the East Asian Development Company with a timber concession on the Yalu River, urged upon Nicholas a recklessly intransigent line that was exemplified by the jingoistic patriotism of their leader, Alexander Bezobrazov. Their bellicose interest in northern Korea, coupled with what seemed to be calculated delay in evacuating Russian troops from Manchuria, convinced the Japanese that their interests were threatened on both fronts, and that whatever the Russians might say about wanting to avoid war was belied by their aggressive actions.

The tsar himself was now (August 1903) in a mood to respond decisively to those who claimed that Russian policy lacked unity and direction, but his response was guided by the Bezobrazov group, who believed that the real problem was a lack of nerve. Parting with Finance Minister Witte, who had always counselled against adventurism, Nicholas decided to forge ahead on his own. To escape further ministerial interference, he elevated a senior naval officer, Admiral Evgenii Alekseev, to the position of Viceroy of the Far East, making him answerable not only for the governance of the region, but also for relations between Russia, Japan, and China. The appointment understandably caused consternation in St Petersburg, where ministers and bureaucrats rightly believed they had been outflanked, and also in Tokyo, where it was seen as heralding further Russian efforts to obtain a Korean seaport, and as making a negotiated settlement of existing differences even less likely. Six months later, the Japanese, having abandoned the diplomatic table, staged a successful surprise attack on the Port Arthur naval base (26 January 1904). With the Russians 'scandalously unprepared' [58 *p. 238*], the results were devastating: several capital ships were torpedoed as they lay at anchor, while a Japanese blockade of the harbour neutralized the remaining ships of the Pacific fleet. Two Russian attempts to break the blockade ended in failure, and by July the Japanese had Port Arthur under siege from both land and sea. The war that Nicholas kept insisting he did not want had already started [63, 68, 73].

DISASTERS IN MANCHURIA

Once hostilities began, St Petersburg was soon awash in sentiments ranging from patriotic enthusiasm to outrageously boastful swaggering [*Doc. 10*]. The tsar himself openly expressed the racial contempt that many Russians felt when he referred to the Japanese as *makaki* (macaques, short-tailed monkeys), and predicted that Russian soldiers would make short work of such an uncivilized nation. The realities of war soon proved him wrong. For one thing, except for a few skirmishes in Turkestan, the Russians had not made war since the 1870s, whereas the Japanese had only recently defeated China, learning in the process a great deal about the logistical requirements of mounting a campaign on the Asian mainland. When the war began, almost all of the men, weapons and supplies that Russia would need in Manchuria were in European Russia, and the only route to the east was the still unfinished and technically inferior Trans-Siberian railway. For a few weeks, the still frozen surface of Lake Baikal could be crossed on hastily laid tracks, but once the thaw began, all transport had to go by steamer while the section along the south shore of the lake was rushed to completion. To the problems of inadequate transport and poor communications were added other complications: provision for the wounded was inadequate, and care had to be hastily improvised by the military, the Russian Red Cross, and a national zemstvo organization specially authorized by the tsar for this purpose; enteric diseases were also a serious problem because Russian soldiers, encouraged by their commanders to disregard the advice of medical officers, were notoriously careless about drinking impure water. Amid much publicity the tsar's mother, Dowager Empress Marie, sent to the front a gleaming and beautifully appointed hospital train, but a more useful gift might have been the simple water testing devices that were used by Japanese medical officers to determine suitable bivouac locations for their soldiers. In marked contrast to the Russians, the Japanese army lost so little of its fighting strength to disease and infection that the other great powers were anxious to copy its techniques and incorporate them into their military planning.

Now that they enjoyed undisputed command of the seas, the Japanese occupied the Korean peninsula, intending to send their troops into Manchuria. The Russians might conceivably have halted this advance at the Yalu, but instead a disagreement between Alexeev and the Commander of the Manchurian Army, General Alexis Kuropatkin, prevented decisive action. After a six-month siege, and in order to avoid further loss of life, the Russian commander of Port Arthur surrendered to the Japanese in December, 1904, a highly controversial action for which he was later court martialled on the grounds that the ammunition, provisions, and other supplies still in the fortress would have sustained the besieged garrison for at least another month. After the Manchurian army made three unsuccessful attempts to stop the Japanese advance, Nicholas finally removed Alexeev and gave Kuropatkin complete control, but the latter was forced to abandon the heavily-fortified city of Mukden (February, 1905) after an extremely bloody battle that lasted for almost three weeks. Now it was Kuropatkin's turn to be relieved of command, although the Japanese forces were by this time stretched to the limit and unable to press home their advantage. Despite the respite, Russia experienced a fresh disgrace when the hastily reorganized Baltic fleet, after a trouble-ridden voyage lasting several months, was defeated in a matter of hours on 14 May in the Straits of Tsushima. The few Russian ships not sunk in this disastrous engagement with the wily Admiral Togo attempted to seek refuge in Vladivostok, but were forced to surrender ten days later [58].

After the Mukden defeat, President Theodore Roosevelt of the United States – another imperial power with an interest in Pacific affairs – attempted to persuade the belligerents to submit to mediation. With the Trans-Siberian railway finally functioning to the Russians' advantage, enabling them to build up reinforcements and supplies far more rapidly than in the early months of the war, the tsar was less ready than the now almost exhausted Japanese to accept Roosevelt's offer. The Tsushima disaster, coupled with the prospect of further domestic disorders, changed the Russian attitude, and negotiations began under American auspices. The Japanese at first tried hard to extract an indemnity from the Russians, and demanded in addition the cession of the island of Sakhalin, but the Russian negotiators, led by the ubiquitous Witte, felt strong enough to threaten a resumption of hostilities, and finally the Japanese yielded. Under the terms of the Treaty of Portsmouth (New Hampshire), signed 16/29 August 1905, no war indemnity was paid, and the Russians gave up only the southern half of Sakhalin; however they also lost the entire Liaotung peninsula, including the South Manchurian railway line, and Port Arthur itself.

Even the tsar's most understanding biographer has concluded that this 'disastrous and unnecessary war with Japan was more Nicholas's fault than anybody else's' [60 *p. 100*]. Inevitably the war, and his personal responsibility for it, became an important ingredient in the growing social and political discontent in St Petersburg and Moscow. Critics of the regime now argued that the autocracy had blundered into a war that the country was ill-equipped to fight, and that Russian soldiers were as much the victims of political incompetence as of foreign aggression. Newspapers heightened the tension with their fevered coverage of the besieged population of Port Arthur, terrorized by repeated artillery bombardment from General Nogi's army. Amid this atmosphere of crisis, more and more Russians began to call for substantial changes in the political structure of the country. The future of the autocracy itself was at stake.

TOWARDS 'BLOODY SUNDAY'

Plehve had come to symbolize all the negative aspects of the existing political order, and his assassination on 15 July 1904 presented the tsar with a clear choice: either to reaffirm it, or to make substantial changes. His inclination was naturally the former, but with his advisers and confidantes divided in their advice, his mother's plea for conciliation apparently struck home. When he chose as Plehve's successor Prince Sviatopolk-Mirskii, an aristocrat of moderate views and honourable intentions, those who believed the autocracy capable of reforming itself took heart. Mirskii immediately, if vaguely, promised reforms, and began to talk about creating a new atmosphere of confidence. The Liberationists were sceptical and the traditionalists apprehensive, but moderate opinion welcomed his new approach, hoping that it would permeate not only the Ministry of the Interior but the government as a whole. Mirskii himself believed, naively but no doubt sincerely, that the tsar was now ready to consider a reform programme that included greater consultation with the public on government policy and legislation, civil rights, more autonomy for local government, and a measure of religious toleration. For a brief moment, it seemed that a consensus for reform might be reached.

Over the next few months the full extent of Mirskii's political innocence became apparent: not only had he badly misjudged Nicholas II, but he soon found himself under attack from both ends of the political spectrum. At a secret meeting in Paris in early October, 1904, most of the revolutionaries and leftwing liberals had already committed themselves to nothing less than the eventual destruction of the autocracy and its replacement by a democratically elected government that would proceed to dismantle the existing Russian Empire [16]. In Russia, the Liberationists adopted an openly revolutionary programme, demanding a constituent assembly elected by universal suffrage, compulsory expropriation (albeit with compensation) of privately owned land, and the introduction of an eight-hour working day. When Mirskii approached them to explore the possibilities for compromise, Miliukov made it plain that there were 'no intermediary positions between autocracy and consistent constitutionalism.' [39 *p.213*]. In reality, such an accommodation was almost inconceivable: the Liberationists had treated Mirskii's appointment as a signal to step up rather than soften their campaign for a constitutional regime, and were in no mood to retreat.

Meanwhile, the zemstvo liberals, over a hundred of whom met in St. Petersburg from 6 to 9 November, were moving to a position well to the left of Shipov's cautious reformism. Fearful that the congress would exceed the bounds of the permissible, Mirskii had first tried to limit its agenda, then to delay it, then to move it to the provinces; eventually he agreed to turn a blind eye if the meeting were private and unofficial. In fact it was anything but private: press reports and hastily telegraphed messages ensured that its proceedings were speedily and widely known. After approving calls for civil liberties, the rule of law, and the democratization of zemstvo elections, delegates considered a proposal for the establishment of an elected, representative legislative body. Shipov tried to rally support for his position, which blamed the bureaucracy for Russia's ills, rejected written constitutions, and endorsed a purely consultative assembly, but on the crucial ballot he mustered only about a quarter of the votes. Evidently the majority were determined to place the rule of law upon much firmer foundations than the trust and moral principles which Shipov thought both essential and sufficient. Yet these 'delegates' were virtually all zemstvo officials and self-appointed activists who had chosen to attend; had they been representatives elected by zemstvo assembly members, Shipov's more moderate position might have suited them better. This possibility was, however, completely lost amid the excitement created by news reports that a national zemstvo congress had strongly endorsed the need for constitutional government in Russia.

With the political temperature obviously rising, defenders of the autocracy rallied to sabotage Mirskii's far more modest proposals for involving elected representatives of the public in the preliminary discussion of proposed legislation. Predictably, both Pobedonostsev and Grand Duke Sergei were vociferous in their opposition, as was Witte, who warned the tsar that Mirskii's proposals were dangerous concessions which would lead inevitably to full constitutional government [60]. Easily persuaded, Nicholas reaffirmed his opposition to any form of representative government, yet characteristically retained in office a minister whose programme he had now clearly rejected. Once rumours to this effect began to circulate among the educated and politically aware, the intransigent constitutionalist position of Miliukov and the Liberationists appeared to make even greater sense; in these events and perceptions lay the real beginnings of the Revolution of 1905 [16].

Throughout Russia and the wider world, however, attention focused on a far more dramatic event: the appalling spectacle of 'Bloody Sunday' (9 January, 1905), when soldiers killed or wounded hundreds of workers who were marching peacefully towards Winter Palace Square in St Petersburg to deliver 'A Most Humble and Loyal Address' to the tsar [*Doc. 11*]. Inevitably, parallels were drawn with the Khodynka disaster, not least because many of the victims belonged to the ostensibly monarchist Assembly of Russian Workers, led by a popular priest, Father George Gapon. Once again it appeared that the tsarist regime was both heartless and criminally negligent in treating loyal subjects with such brutality.

'Bloody Sunday' was indisputably a massacre, but sharply drawn moral judgements explain little about the actions of the authorities, the workers, or indeed Gapon himself. Aware that the Liberationists planned to use strikes and demonstrations to further their cause, the government was nevertheless caught by surprise when a strike that began at the huge Putilov munitions works spread so quickly that by January 7 well over half of the city's factory workers had come out in support. On learning that Gapon was organizing a march to present a petition to the tsar, authorities decided both to ban the procession, and to prevent Gapon or his workers from entering the centre of the city, holding to these decisions despite last-minute pleas from alarmed citizens who feared possible bloodshed. Arguably, the deployment of infantry units armed only with rifles, inexplicable when cavalry units had also been put on alert, almost guaranteed that a massacre would take place when such an enormous crowd materialized. Although the membership of Gapon's Russian Assembly cannot have exceeded 20,000 at most, far more than that number – perhaps as many as 100,000 workers – joined the march that day. Because they followed a priest, carrying icons and portraits of the tsar, their level of political consciousness has been questioned by some historians [109]. It was also questioned at the time by both Bolsheviks and Mensheviks, who thought the whole scheme wrong-headed, but others objected to characterizing them as 'superstitious dolts' simply because they were ignorant of Marxist revolutionary theory [16 *p. 84*]. Gapon himself was idiosyncratic in matters of religion as well as politics: the special mission that he felt to minister to the urban poor led him first to seek funds and protection from Zubatov while organizing his Assembly, then to develop the far more extreme political views that, among other things, soon brought him into contact with the Liberationists, who believed that through him they could reach the workers. Once the strike began to spread, he became convinced that destiny called him to bring together the Russian people and their tsar, despite the fact that his petition called for an elected constituent assembly, the legalization of trade unions, and many other reforms that were anathema to Nicholas II, who in any case chose to spend this fateful day elsewhere.

While foreign diplomats posted to St Petersburg marvelled at the regime's incompetence and foreign newspapers reacted with exaggerated outrage, Russians themselves tried to come to terms with the violence of 'Bloody Sunday'. The government, predictably, sought to discredit Gapon – Pobedonostsev ingeniously blamed the whole affair on agitators from abroad – but in many places workers joined the strike movement in even greater numbers, students staged strikes and demonstrations of their own, zemstvo assemblies were radicalized overnight, and the Liberationists sought to turn to political advantage the growing revulsion against the tsar and his ministers. Within the next four months, news of the defeats at Mukden and Tsushima – further confirmation of the regime's incompetence – only added to the outrage over 'Bloody Sunday'. The opposition believed that such morally indefensible violence would discredit its perpetrators and so force fundamental and permanent political changes of which they would be the beneficiaries. Many liberals and radicals were therefore caught by surprise when official violence begat popular violence, a veritable explosion of unruly behaviour that, within a year, so altered the Russian political landscape as to make possible the survival of the tsarist regime, a prospect that seemed inconceivable on the morning after 'Bloody Sunday'.

AWAKENINGS: THE REVOLUTIONARY YEAR 1905

'Russia in Disarray', the subtitle of an important recent book on the Revolution of 1905, catches exactly the confusion and disorder throughout the whole empire that marked this year at every level of society [16]. Thanks to Sergei Eisenstein's brilliantly partisan film, the mutiny on the battleship Potemkin has become perhaps the best-known event of the year, which is ironic because it was manifest disaffection in the army, rather than mutiny in the fleet, that so concerned the tsarist regime during this revolutionary year [27]. Nevertheless, the Potemkin mutiny is a useful symbol of the degree to which, for months on end, the familiar Russian world was turned upside-down, challenging the customary relations of authority and deference. Workers defied foremen and employers; students and professors, the university authorities; peasants, rural landowners and supervisory officials; borderland peoples, their Russian overlords. The Potemkin's hated officers jumped or were cast overboard; in similar incidents on land, petty autocrats of all kinds, from factory foremen to chief hospital surgeons, often found themselves subjected to unceremonious wheelbarrow rides, in all likelihood to the nearest foul ditch or dunghill.

Peasants, students, workers and national minorities were no strangers to unrest; the novelty here lay not in the kind but the degree of disruption. However, some of the other manifestations of unruliness appeared to be unprecedented: parish priests criticizing the Church hierarchy, artisans and apprentices speaking out on civic matters as well as employment issues, women workers voicing grievances against male co-workers and bosses, liberal and socialist feminists attacking male privilege. Suddenly, groups of people who had not previously contemplated such a step were forming unions and associations; soon these bodies held meetings, debated issues, held congresses, passed resolutions, and started publishing their own newsletters and journals. In place of established, top-down authority (*nachalstvo**), many newly articulate groups took as their watchword *samodeiatelnost,** a term already used in zemstvo and professional circles to mean activity spontaneously initiated and autonomously directed, free from interference by agents of the Russian state. The entire country, it seemed, was caught up in a continuous swirl of unaccustomed and frenzied activity.

The pace of these events was set from below, and for most of the year the government found it impossible to regain control over the activities of the populace, many of whom were beginning to behave more like articulate citizens than deferential subjects. Although the government attempted to take various initiatives in the succeeding months, everything it did was either too little, too late, or hopelessly inappropriate. For example, Nicholas II, having refused to meet Gapon's marchers, finally received a hand-picked delegation of workers, not in order to express regret for the massacre, but to give them the message that their deluded fellow-strikers would be forgiven only if such events were not repeated. In late January, the government sensibly moved to establish a committee of inquiry to investigate and report on labour discontent in St Petersburg and, extending an unexpected olive branch, even provided for worker-elected representatives on the committee itself; yet this came to naught when the government refused workers' demands for guarantees that their representatives would not be liable to prosecution or subjected to violence while performing their duties. No doubt these and other demands reflected the growing influence of the Social Democrats, especially the Mensheviks who, having played no part in Gapon's organization, were now determined to set their stamp on the labour movement, but the main reason for the government's refusal lay elsewhere. In mid-February, the tsar had made what he thought of as the ultimate gesture of reconciliation: he conceded that elected representatives of the public might indeed be involved in the preliminary consideration of legislative proposals. Because this was the very issue on which Mirskii had found him intransigent, the sincerity of this concession was immediately questioned by critics on both ends of the political spectrum. As for Nicholas, he made it clear that after deciding of his own volition to take such a magnanimous step, he would brook no further attempts to dictate conditions to his government.

The Liberationists, now faced with the prospect of a merely consultative body, redoubled their efforts to force the calling of a constituent assembly, using for this purpose a broader vehicle known as the Union of Unions. Formed in early May – only days before Russians learned of the Tsushima disaster – under the leadership of Professor Miliukov, the Union of Unions brought together fourteen national 'unions' of professionals and intellectuals, including lawyers, engineers, medical personnel, pharmacists, academics, writers, and teachers. A loose umbrella organization, it also included Unions for Jewish Equality and for the Equality of Women, a Union of Railway Employees, and even a Union of Zemstvo-Constitutionalists, whose members became uneasy when some of the more outspoken professionals expressed extremely radical views [39, 87]. By June, when the Union of Unions held a second congress, Miliukov had decided that there was no longer a place for the 'parlour constitutionalism' of the moderates [16 *p. 144*]; he himself proposed a fully revolutionary course of action, sanctioning all methods of struggle, including a general strike, until the regime had been brought to its knees. This was too much for the moderates who, now convinced that Miliukov had abandoned liberalism altogether, left the Union of Unions to its radical fate.

The promise of a consultative assembly that would no doubt be dominated by the privileged meant little or nothing to those segments of Russian society for whom 1905 was a remarkable year of political awakening. Ferment in the villages, in most cases led by peasants themselves rather than by local schoolteachers or SR agitators, led to the creation of an All-Russian Peasants' Union which, meeting at a congress in July, called for the abolition of the private ownership of land. All over Russia, voices from 'the lower depths' became not only audible but insistent. Laundresses and cleaners who suddenly demanded a say in the running of hospitals had their counterparts in the lowly railway greasemen who began to speak up for workers' rights, the women factory workers who demanded an end to body searches and other forms of sexual harassment in the workplace, and the exploited miners who refused to risk their lives in the appalling conditions to which most of their employers were utterly indifferent. What needs underlining here is that, all over the country, the possibility of change at the local level was perceived to be directly connected to a sweeping transformation of authority and its exercise at the national level. Thus the demands for constitutional government and civil rights that came from every quarter were not so much evidence of mass conversion to the ideals of liberalism and parliamentary government as they were demands for an end to privilege, arbitrary behaviour and oppression in the workplace and the village, as well as in the school, the university, and perhaps even the family itself. There was a universal sense that a watershed had been reached; that life at all levels could no longer be lived as it had been, and that a new order of things had to be constructed.

Although these awakenings usually took place among groups lacking in privilege and authority, they were certainly not confined to them; those with considerably more to lose were awakened just as effectively, albeit more rudely, once they realized that the government's authority was faltering, and hence could no longer be counted upon to provide protection against the clamour of popular agitation. Until 1905, Russian businessmen had been largely untouched by the growth of liberalism in zemstvo, academic and professional circles, but now leading figures in commerce and industry entered the national debate about the future of Russia; inevitably, this development has led historians to ask whether 'the missing middle class' had finally arrived on the Russian scene? [19, 29]. If by this one means a class-conscious bourgeoisie in the Marxian sense, then the answer is surely negative; for although industrialists and the scions of Moscow merchant houses formed local and national organizations, published newspapers, and spoke out on political issues, most of them quickly abandoned their brief and belated enthusiasm for dramatic political and social change. During the summer months, as industrial and urban unrest grew, compounded by disturbances in the countryside and disorder in the borderlands, businessmen quickly retreated from tepid constitutionalism to an obsession with law and order that was far more consistent with the conservative nationalism that traditionally characterized Moscow's commercial and industrial leaders [74]. This concern for the restoration of order was also shared by die-hard monarchists who believed that the tsar was failing to win the battle against liberals and socialists because he was receiving untrustworthy advice, especially from (the recently ennobled) Count Witte. This sudden awakening on the political right began in February, as soon as Nicholas promised a consultative duma; needless to say it gained strength in October, when Witte counselled further concessions. Though principally the creation of Russian landowners, the awakening on the right soon tapped into anti-Polish and anti-Jewish sentiment in the western provinces and the Ukraine, producing a number of rightist political parties whose extremism and popular appeal were chiefly a function of their antisemitism [85].

A NEW CONSTITUTION?

In August, hoping to regain the initiative, the government published the electoral law for the consultative assembly promised earlier. Peasants, landowners and propertied townsmen constituted the entire eligible electorate; women, Jews, young men, non-Russians, and the urban and rural poor were all excluded [94]. Not surprisingly, the law's restrictions fuelled rather than allayed discontent, and the next two months produced renewed strikes in both capitals and many provincial centres. Although working-class unity and solidarity should not be overestimated, there is no doubt that the railwaymen, who sent trainloads of agitators and organizers around the country, helped to spread the strike movement and sometimes provoked peasants into revolutionary actions [33, 87, 97]. With the Union of Unions as well as leading Russian liberals supporting the strike movement, and conservatives near panic lest rebellion spread to the borderlands and mass insubordination to the army and the fleet, the tsarist regime reached an unprecedented crisis point in mid-October, when Nicholas II, desperate for a way out, once again sought the advice of Count Witte.

Witte believed that the situation called for either the imposition of a military dictatorship or the granting of further significant constitutional concessions. Both courses were risky, but Witte advised the latter, not because he had suddenly been converted to liberalism and parliamentary government, but because this course offered the possibility of dividing the regime's non-revolutionary opponents from their more militant allies. Some of the regime's leading critics, Miliukov, for example, were politicians-in-waiting, longing for the opportunity to organize and lead a real political party, to campaign and participate in a legal election, to make speeches from the rostrum of a national assembly, and to publish newspapers containing editorials as well as their speeches for all to read. Witte knew that the promise of a legislature would not persuade Miliukov to call off his war on the autocracy, but it would put that war on a different footing, and the regime could easily benefit from the inevitable pause while the locus of liberal opposition shifted from the streets to the hustings and then to the Duma itself [50, 71, 113]. With great reluctance Nicholas II accepted Witte's advice, and on 17 October 1905 issued a manifesto proclaiming his intention to institute fundamental civil liberties, to extend the franchise more widely, and to make all new laws subject to the approval of the Duma. Soon afterwards he wrote, 'My dearest Mama, you can't imagine what I went through before that moment . . . There was no other way out than to cross oneself and give what everyone was asking for' [60 *p. 149*]. As this frank confession reveals, it was desperation, not conviction, that led Nicholas to take this extraordinary step. Nevertheless, when news of the tsar's decision reached the Liberationists in Paris, Struve became ecstatic [*Doc. 12*].

The October Manifesto may not have been the panacea that Nicholas II hoped for, but its publication did significantly alter the situation confronting the government. Just as important as the liberals' willingness to appeal to the electorate and transfer the struggle to the floor of the Duma was the fact that many moderate unions, the railwaymen being the most important, decided that this was the moment for a return to work; more intransigent workers who still remained on strike now faced the possibility of lockouts by employers impatient to see order restored. On the other hand, resistance – some of it considerable – continued long after the manifesto was issued, and much blood was shed in the effort to suppress it. In St Petersburg, a general strike was organized and directed by a Soviet (Council) of Workers' Deputies; this body survived until the government counterattacked in early December, arresting its leaders and dissolving the Soviet, and then dealing with the armed uprisings that these moves provoked in Moscow and other cities [22, 109]. Among the borderland nationalities, in the army and navy, and especially among the peasantry, disorders continued well into 1906; the government responded by sending punitive expeditions to mete out brutal and exemplary punishments [27, 101]. Although some claimed that Russia was on the threshold of a new era of constitutional government, those in authority gave no sign of abandoning the traditional, forceful responses to disorder that were euphemistically referred to as 'pacification'.

The revolutionary flame, after burning so brightly, soon began to sputter. Remarkably, a mere six months after publishing the October Manifesto, the government gambled that further concessions were unlikely, and that it could begin to modify some of those already made. By April, 1906, when the necessary revisions to the Fundamental Laws were published, considerable backtracking had already taken place. Although the manifesto had promised that no new law could take effect without the approval of the State Duma, whole areas of government activity – foreign policy, defence, the Imperial Court – were declared to be exclusive prerogatives of the sovereign and hence placed beyond the jurisdiction of the Duma. Moreover, in a virtual invitation to constitutional abuse, a soon-to-be infamous clause (Article 87) gave the government power to proclaim laws when the Duma was not in session, subject to later ratification by the legislative body. Finally, although the manifesto had made no mention of a bicameral legislature, the April revisions called for a largely appointed upper house to exercise legislative power equally with the Duma; this body was simply a refurbishing of the existing State Council, with the addition of some members elected by corporate bodies such as the universities, the Academy of Sciences, and commercial-industrial organizations. The net effect of all these changes was to deliver much less than the manifesto had promised, and the government breathed a sigh of relief when its actions evoked no significant protests or disturbances. The liberals were naturally infuriated by this back-door manoeuvring, but were now scarcely in a position to resume open struggle with the government. Whether an appeal to the people at this point would have provoked renewed disturbances is doubtful; the issues involved were not easily explained to an untutored electorate. In any case, most liberals were already preoccupied with the forthcoming convocation of the First Duma, so they decided that securing redress for these 'broken promises' would become part of their legislative agenda.

5 REVIVAL OF NERVE, 1907–1914

THE ELUSIVE COMPROMISE

Implementing the October Manifesto raised a host of difficult questions. For a functioning constitutional monarchy to emerge from the turmoil of 1905, compromises would be required on all sides. Would Nicholas II accept the new Duma as a legitimate part of the apparatus of government? Could he find and work with a prime minister who was ready to do the same? Were ministers and senior officials prepared to adapt to a new political environment, or would they attempt to emasculate or even scuttle the new legislative body? Would the reformed State Council play a useful and co-operative role as a chamber of sober second thought, or would it defeat or delay every measure that was sent to it by the lower house? Were the newly-formed political parties prepared to work with the government, or would they all simply use the Duma as a political grandstand? Finally, even if a political compromise of some sort could be hammered out, would the resulting legislation deal constructively with the most important problems facing the country? The answers to many of these questions emerged between 1906 and 1909.

The political atmosphere was hardly conducive to compromise, and nothing demonstrates this more clearly than the fate of Shipov, the respected erstwhile leader of the zemstvo-constitutionalists. He believed that the October Manifesto opened the door to the reconstruction of Russia, and sought to make confrontation a thing of the past by rallying support for a new era of constructive activity. To this end he founded the Union of 17 October (Octobrists), which he envisioned as a patriotic league rather than a political organization designed for partisan combat. To his mind, any individual or organization prepared to co-operate with the government on the basis of the manifesto could shelter under the Octobrist umbrella, but he soon discovered that only a handful of Russians shared his distaste for partisan politics. On the left, the Constitutional Democrats (nicknamed

Kadets) and the various socialist parties assumed that the manifesto had merely changed the terrain on which they would continue their struggle against tsarism; while on the right, new parties such as the ultra-nationalist and openly antisemitic Union of the Russian People planned to use the Duma to attack exponents of 'foreign' ideologies such as liberalism and socialism, hoping thereby to discredit constitutionalism and restore unlimited autocracy. Paradoxically, among the fledgling groups of political moderates, Shipov's programme quickly attracted advocates of law and order who sought to transform the Octobrists into a party that would defend the interests of property-owners and support the cause of Russian imperialism at home and abroad. Prominent among them were Alexander Guchkov, the flamboyant scion of a Moscow commercial family, and Michael Rodzianko, a wealthy landowner from the Ukraine; they aligned the Octobrists firmly behind the government's forcible restoration of order in the countryside, and denounced supporters of Polish and Finnish autonomy for attempting to destroy the Russian Empire. Most Octobrists found this strident rhetoric to their liking, and when the increasingly isolated and uncomfortable Shipov resigned the leadership in April, 1906, they chose Guchkov as his successor. In desperation, Shipov founded a Party of Peaceful Renovation, but in this era of political antagonism it was doomed to impotence.

Another possible avenue of compromise was briefly touted: the formation of a so-called 'ministry of confidence' in which a few eminent individuals from outside the bureaucracy might be given ministerial office. Some saw this as a genuine attempt to build a bridge between officialdom and civil society, while others dismissed it as a cynical attempt to emasculate the Duma by co-opting the nonrevolutionary opposition. Although more than one attempt was made to reach this goal through secret negotiations, Nicholas II was lukewarm to the idea; conceivably he might have been persuaded to invite Shipov to join the government, but – as the latter admitted – a coalition formed without the participation of leading liberals would have little credibility, and at this juncture Miliukov haughtily dismissed any idea of co-operating with the government. Now leader of the Kadets, Miliukov was convinced that these secret overtures only proved the weakness of the tsarist regime, so he held out for a ministry responsible to the Duma majority, which he confidently expected to lead [8, 90]. In later years, he was castigated for intransigence by more pragmatic liberals, but theirs was a dubious argument given the tsar's unyielding conviction that he understood the true desires of the Russian people far better than the liberals, whom he dismissed as self-promoting politicians animated by delusions of grandeur. In the circumstances, a coalition ministry was clearly not a practical means of restoring public confidence in the government [60, 71, 82].

Nicholas II was appalled when the Kadets emerged from the elections as the most numerous party in the First Duma, with 182 out of 448 deputies; indeed, some three-quarters of the deputies were members of the liberal or radical opposition [32]. The Bolsheviks had boycotted the elections, but about one-third of the deputies belonged to three other left-wing parties (Mensheviks, SRs, and Labourites [*Trudoviki*]); various centre parties managed to elect no more than forty-four deputies, while nationalist and rightist parties had sixty-eight adherents. In contrast to the tsar, Miliukov was elated by the results, and believed that this was the moment to beat the regime into submission. On the eve of the Duma's convocation – set for 27 April 1906 – the tsar, faced with the prospect of more political turbulence, suddenly dismissed the energetic but unruly Witte from the Chairmanship of the Council of Ministers, replacing him with Ivan Goremykin, an aging and obedient bureaucrat who was unlikely to work towards any sort of accommodation with the Duma. His appointment was regarded as a deliberate provocation by most deputies, especially the Kadets, who used the rostrum of the Duma to condemn the government, lecture the ministers, and (as they thought) rally support for their party by calling for land expropriation, a political amnesty, ministerial responsibility, and an end to arbitrary and bureaucratic government. When Goremykin made no positive response on any of these issues and explicitly ruled out the expropriation of private land, many deputies boldly decided to communicate directly with the people; from the relative safety of Vyborg, just across the Finnish border, they composed an address to the population. The government quickly condemned this 'clearly illegal' act and, in order to teach the upstart deputies a lesson, it dissolved the Duma (8 July 1906) and called for new elections. Although elected for a five-year term, the First Duma had lasted scarcely more than two months. Only convinced reactionaries thought this was the moment to abolish the Duma completely, but there was a notable absence of public protest over the dissolution itself [*Doc. 13*]. In the countryside, however, peasants who had expected the Duma to present them with the nobles' land vented their frustration in a fresh wave of arson and disorder.

The election results dispelled any hope that the Second Duma would prove more tractable than its predecessor. Almost half of its members belonged to the socialist parties to the left of the Kadets, whose own numbers were reduced to fewer than a hundred deputies.

Many prominent Kadets were disqualified from participating because they had signed the so-called Vyborg Manifesto urging peasants to refuse tax payments and recruits as a gesture of protest against the dissolution of the First Duma. This was, however, not the only reason for the Kadets' poorer showing. Peasant voters sent more radical deputies to the Second Duma because they wanted quick, dramatic action on the land question, and believed that their interests would be better served by socialists than by liberals. Thus the Kadets found themselves sandwiched uncomfortably between the firebrands of the left and those of the right, disparaged by the former for their obsession with legality and pilloried by the latter for their refusal to condemn terrorism outright. Despite (or perhaps because of) the Second Duma's radical complexion, the government took a somewhat more conciliatory approach, but it too failed to produce a more co-operative atmosphere.

The new initiative was the work of Peter Stolypin, a noble landowner turned provincial governor, whose impressive handling of the revolutionary crisis had led Nicholas to appoint him Minister of the Interior in April, 1906. A political pragmatist, Stolypin was convinced that the regime's survival depended upon the support of the nonrevolutionary opposition, and that it was therefore essential for the government to build a working relationship with the legislature [53]. Braving the hostile atmosphere of the Second Duma, he deliberately replaced Goremykin's studied indifference with a firm commitment to introduce specific reforms in several areas, especially local government and land tenure [62]. Stolypin professed to believe in a government based on law, but most deputies found this claim contradictory, if not outrageously hypocritical, given his public defence of the field courts martial authorized by the tsar to dispense summary and usually bloody justice to those suspected of arson or other disturbances in the countryside [17, 27]. In any case, his proposals for agrarian reform stopped well short of the modified form of land expropriation now advocated by the Kadets, and even the moderate Octobrists were no longer unanimous in supporting the government's repressive measures. Realizing that there was little likelihood of creating a centrist majority in the Second Duma, Stolypin concocted a pretext for its dissolution, and rewrote the electoral law to ensure that its successor would be more malleable. This step, immediately condemned as a *coup d'état* by the opposition, was in effect a confession that genuine political compromise had eluded the government, which was now prepared to contrive a substitute.

THE STOLYPIN YEARS

A new stage in Russia's experiment in constitutionalism began on 3 June, 1907 with the publication of Stolypin's revised electoral law. Broadly speaking, the goal of the revisions was to increase substantially the electoral weight of the propertied classes at the expense of those less well off; and of Russians at the expense of non-Russians, especially in the borderland areas. On both counts it was a success. When the Third Duma met in November 1907, its composition was startlingly different from its predecessors: the Kadets and the socialists together numbered less than a hundred deputies, while more than three hundred deputies belonged to centre or right-wing parties. Guchkov was now the dominant figure in the Duma, and he made it clear to the 154 Octobrist deputies that whatever their published programme said about constitutionalism and legality, their main tasks were to support and influence the government, and to keep the Kadets and socialists from interfering with the Duma's work. He and Stolypin respected each other both politically and personally, and they looked forward to a period of productive co-operation between government and Duma [43].

Co-operation of sorts there was, but it did not prove durable. Guchkov, now that he was in the political limelight, took the opportunity to press the government hard on matters dear to his heart, especially Russian defence and foreign policy, thereby incurring the enmity of the tsar, who regarded these as matters exclusively within the Imperial prerogative. The Octobrist leader, following his own political agenda, urged the Duma to delay approval of a naval shipbuilding programme that many considered essential after the Tsushima disaster; denounced the Grand Dukes – Nicholas' relatives – for exercising a malignant influence on the army; and openly criticized Russia's diplomatic collapse when Austria demanded that other powers recognize its formal annexation of the Balkan territory of Bosnia-Herzegovina. Undoubtedly the War Minister, General Rediger, tacitly supported Guchkov's attack on the tsar's interfering uncles; he and his officials hoped to use the Duma to pressure the Finance Ministry into providing greater support for modernizing the army, and to escape from the policing role that had been forced upon unwilling generals during the 1905–06 disruptions [38]. By 1909, after the tsar refused to approve a defence-related appropriation bill because the Duma, at Guchkov's urging, had dared to discuss its contents, Stolypin realized that if he wished to retain the tsar's confidence he would have to forsake either the Octobrists or the Duma itself. Meanwhile the tsar began searching for a less unreliable war minister.

Steering a course between Guchkov's unpredictability and the tsar's easily wounded pride was only one of Stolypin's headaches. In 1906 he announced a sweeping reform of local government that sought to expand zemstvo institutions, activities, and budgets, albeit under the watchful supervision of the central government. His proposals proved highly controversial. Sceptics in the bureaucracy doubted the wisdom as well as the feasibility of his plan. Advocates of zemstvo autonomy favoured his intention to broaden the electoral law and establish local zemstvos at the cantonal level, but they were understandably alarmed by the prospect of closer bureaucratic supervision. While they floundered, Russia's noble landowners mounted a campaign aimed at forcing the premier to modify or, preferably, abandon his plan for reforming local government. Widespread rural unrest in 1905–06 had compelled the nobles to realize that they could not depend on the government to defend their interests, and the recent relaxation of restrictions on organized activity enabled them to form what was in effect a strong lobby group, the Congress of Representatives of Nobles' Associations, or 'United Nobility' [21, 30, 46]. Politically well to the right of the Octobrists, the nobles opposed the reform in part because they thought Stolypin was misguided in his attempt to reach an accommodation with Duma moderates, and in part because they feared that their leading position in local affairs would be jeopardized by the establishment of a democratized cantonal zemstvo [64, 115]. Above all, they feared that unsophisticated peasant electors would be easily led astray by members of the rural intelligentsia, the school teachers and zemstvo physicians whose 'disloyalty' had been manifest in 1905 [37, 99]. Using their influence among like-minded ministers and officials, in provincial zemstvo assemblies, at the Imperial Court, and especially in the State Council, the United Nobility forced Stolypin to backtrack. In a striking concession, he promised to create within the Interior Ministry a new body, dominated by nobles and their sympathizers, that would screen all measures concerning local government before they were sent to the Duma. As a result, the nobles were largely able to thwart the premier's intentions, staving off both the introduction of more democratic local zemstvos, and the proposed expansion of zemstvo activities. Ironically, one indisputable consequence of the Revolution of 1905 was a significant increase in the political power of nobles, welcome at a time when increasing economic problems threatened to destroy their privileged position in Russian society.

Stolypin fared better with his proposals for agrarian reform, which were supported not only by Guchkov and the Octobrists, who believed that they would modernize the countryside, but also by the nobility, who hoped to preserve the existing social order by defusing the peasants' revolutionary potential [115]. Before 1905, economic arguments against communal agriculture, with its periodic redistribution of separated strips, had foundered on the belief, popular among officials, that the commune was a bulwark of peasant conservatism. When the turmoil of 1905–06 proved otherwise, forcing the government to abandon further attempts to collect redemption dues, the way was cleared for sweeping changes. Stolypin's goal was to create a new class of peasant proprietors who would be both hardworking and politically reliable; private ownership, he believed, would fire their ambition and give them an excellent reason to care about the future political stability of the country. He therefore introduced legislation making it possible for peasant households to separate from the commune and become private owners of their share of its land; these new owners were also encouraged to consolidate their scattered strips into contiguous farmsteads – a move which Stolypin expected to promote more efficient and productive agriculture. In the long run, he assured the radical Second Duma, this approach made much greater economic sense than the expropriation of large estates, a drastic measure that would do little to promote rural harmony while offering no guarantees of increased productivity. Not surprisingly, socialist deputies remained unconvinced, while liberals agonized because the premier had introduced his laws as emergency decrees; the required ratification was not forthcoming until 1910–11, when the Third Duma finally approved the legislation, but by then his reforms were already underway in rural Russia.

Despite a promising beginning, Stolypin's land reform fell short of the admittedly varied expectations of its supporters. The initial burst of enthusiasm lasted until 1909, but thereafter applications from households wishing to separate from the commune began to fall off. A decade after its introduction, only about 20 per cent of eligible households had separated, and only half of those went on to consolidate their holdings. Despite the cheap credit made available through the Peasant Land Bank, few households could afford the costs involved in operating as a consolidated farmstead. The reform had its greatest appeal in the black-soil provinces of southern Russia and the Ukraine where fertility was high, but it was certainly no panacea for the agricultural backwardness of European Russia. Predictions of continuing increases in productivity proved to be overly optimistic, partly because peasant entrepreneurs neglected soil conservation measures in their haste to make a profit. Whether the 'separators' became dependable supporters of the regime remains a matter for conjecture, but it is indisputable that strong resentment built up against them among those peasants who preferred not to risk the limited security that came with commune membership. After the tsarist regime collapsed in 1917, the socially isolated 'Stolypin peasants' quickly became targets for the anger and frustration of their neighbours [42]. As for the nobles' fond hope that this reform would reduce social tensions in rural Russia, it was mere wishful thinking.

The last two years of Stolypin's premiership – he was assassinated in 1911 – were dominated by issues of nationality and Russification. To escape the tsar's hostility towards Guchkov, Stolypin forged a new alliance with the moderate right and nationalist deputies in the Third Duma [30]. Their leader, Count Bobrinskii, urged the government to be fearless in asserting Russian interests within the empire, particularly in those borderland areas where Russian minorities found themselves surrounded by non-Russians. Stolypin had already used the revised electoral law to assert Russian primacy, so he easily took on the role of defending Russia against its internal enemies, an especially attractive course at a moment when his government felt unable to pursue a more aggressive foreign policy.

Once again the Finns were an obvious target. They had taken advantage of the regime's apparent weakness in 1905 to reassert and re-establish the autonomy of the Grand Duchy, and members of the reconstituted Finnish Diet, smarting from the Bobrikov era, were adamant in opposing further interference from the Imperial capital. Inevitably, more clashes occurred, and Stolypin saw an opportunity to settle the Finnish problem in a way that would appeal broadly to Russian nationalists in the Third Duma. He introduced a bill that effectively destroyed Finnish autonomy by reducing the competence of the Diet almost to naught, establishing instead the primacy of Russian laws in virtually every important aspect of public affairs. Adding insult to injury, he reminded the Finns that as subjects of the tsar they were entitled to send representatives to the Duma and the State Council in St Petersburg. On learning that an ultra-nationalist Duma deputy had congratulated his colleagues for terminating Finland's very existence, the Finns redoubled their intransigence. Nothing had been settled by 1914, but the country's strategic importance as well as the increasingly pro-German sentiments of many Finns led the Russians to impose martial law in a desperate attempt to prevent treachery, open rebellion, or secession [111].

Despite playing the nationalist card, Stolypin was starting to lose the confidence of Nicholas II. Already in 1909, the tsar had chosen as his new Minister of War the authoritarian and fiercely independent

General Vladimir Sukhomlinov, who was known to disparage the Premier's working alliance with the Duma. Tensions reached a head in 1911 when the State Council defied Stolypin by rejecting his bill for the creation of zemstvos in the westernmost provinces of the empire, despite the bill's prior approval by the Duma. To please the Nationalists, Stolypin had designed a special electoral system that magnified the importance of the Russian minority at the expense of the predominantly Polish upper class, and it was this feature of the bill that aroused the opposition of traditionalists in the State Council. They believed that such tampering with the privileges of noble landowners, Polish or not, was wrong-headed because it could set a dangerous precedent that might one day be extended to the central Russian provinces. Enraged by their decision, Stolypin insisted that both legislative chambers be prorogued so that the law could be introduced under Article 87. Only with the greatest reluctance did the tsar comply. Having effectively lost faith in the Premier's judgement, Nicholas was nevertheless an appalled eyewitness to Stolypin's assassination at the Kiev opera house in September, 1911, ironically during a performance of Glinka's *A Life for the Tsar*. Neither nationalist nor constitutionalist sentiment motivated his assassin, a former revolutionary who had repented his decision to become a police agent.

RECRIMINATIONS, PURGES, AND SCANDALS

The Stolypin years were a nightmare of frustrated hopes and recriminations for those who had joined or supported the Liberation movement in 1904–05. It was bad enough that the regime had managed to suppress the revolution with arrests, courts martial, and punitive expeditions; it was even worse that it had been able to renege on its promises, dissolve the first two Dumas, and rewrite the electoral law without the slightest sign of a new revolutionary eruption. In 1908, the left reeled at news that a leading SR, Evno Azev, had been exposed as a police spy. The unimaginable had become reality: Russia was now a place where resurgent monarchists, noble landowners, chauvinistic nationalists, and right-wing demagogues were establishing or influencing the political agenda. Erstwhile Liberationists gnashed their teeth, looked for scapegoats, or conducted searching post-mortem examinations on a revolution that was now apparently defunct.

Zemstvo leaders who had promoted resolutions aligning the zemstvos with the Liberation movement were among the first to experience repudiation. A tide of reaction filled provincial zemstvo assemblies with deputies horrified by the violence and social instability that had rocked the countryside [64]. Often they vented their anger on zemstvo employees, especially teachers, medical personnel and other technical experts, many of whom were dismissed outright in what was effectively a purge of radicals [19, 99]. Particularly lively conflicts took place in those professions where a 'union' had been formed as an affiliate of the Union of Unions. Those who had urged that course in 1905 now found themselves condemned for having put political concerns above professional obligations. For example, zemstvo physicians who had argued that an end to tsarist incompetence was a prerequisite for improving public health now found themselves attacked by medical colleagues for having allowed political radicalism to shape questionable professional judgments [54]. Comparable recriminations occurred throughout the professional intelligentsia.

Attacks on radicalism accelerated in 1909. Educated society was astonished when the Liberationist Struve and several other former Marxists published a devastating assault on the assumptions and pretensions of the political intelligentsia [82, 86]. In a remarkable collection of essays called *Landmarks (Vekhi)*, half a dozen of Russia's leading thinkers condemned their fellow intellectuals for arrogance, dogmatism, atheism, intellectual sterility, and – despite their 'cult of the people' – alienation from popular culture [*Doc. 14*]. What they had proven, the essayists agreed, was that they understood neither social change nor the Russian mind. The country's greatest need was to teach the government and the bureaucracy to accept the rule of law, but the intelligentsia had shown that they lacked the moral authority to serve as teachers; thus they were as much to blame as the government for the disaster of 1905–06. Understandably, Russian intellectuals immediately began quarrelling over whether *Landmarks* was brilliant analysis or spiteful self-exoneration; while they did so, academics in Russian universities suffered an equally devastating assault from another quarter.

Seething discontent on university campuses had eventually driven the beleaguered government to make concessions. In August, 1905, 'temporary rules' restored a large measure of the autonomy that faculty and students had enjoyed in the 1860s but subsequently lost [56, 104]. For professors, the two most sensitive issues were the right of academic senates to choose rectors and other senior officials, and the right to fill academic vacancies on the basis of merit. Students claimed the right not only to govern themselves but also to engage in political activity as they saw fit. However, as in so many other areas, the government soon changed course when it realized that the revolutionary force had largely spent itself. Successive Ministers of Education simply ignored the 'temporary rules' and fired rectors, deans, and professors, filling vacancies with their own appointees. As Minister from 1910 to 1914, Leo Kasso, himself a former professor with connections among right-wing academics, outraged students by imposing restrictions on their organizations and relentlessly pursuing those engaged in opposition political activity. When the revered writer Leo Tolstoi died in late 1910, his funeral became the occasion for a huge demonstration in defence of academic freedom and university autonomy. A heavy-handed response from the government only provoked further disorders and strikes, which soon affected almost all universities and higher technical schools. In February, 1911, the exasperated Kasso launched a crackdown on student activists and 'undesirable' or 'lax' professors. This was a full-scale purge: professors were fired and students were subjected to mass expulsions, arrests, and deportations. At the University of Moscow, professors who resigned in a concerted protest against the purge were forced to scramble for teaching jobs elsewhere when the government refused to back down. Rightists praised Kasso when overt campus disturbances appeared to end abruptly, but in reality his crusade gained recruits for the revolutionary underground and soured many professionals whose abilities the regime would soon need in order to cope with the stresses of war.

By 1914, several incidents had cast doubt on the integrity and political judgement of the tsarist regime, thus contributing to the disaffection of educated and privileged Russians. In the Duma, Guchkov waged a virtual vendetta against War Minister Sukhomlinov, whom he accused of a questionable association with an officer suspected of, and subsequently convicted for, being a German spy. More damaging was the ubiquitous gossip about the presence at court of an unkempt and dissolute Siberian peasant named Gregory Rasputin, who had won the gratitude of Nicholas and Alexandra because he possessed an inexplicable but undeniable ability to stop the fearful bleeding of their haemophiliac son, Tsarevich Alexis. Liberals and socialists regarded this so-called 'holy man' as one more in a procession of charlatans and adventurers whose presence at court simply confirmed the moral decay of tsarism, but conservatives were outraged, fearing that his notoriously unsavoury behaviour would discredit the monarchy itself. Stolypin had managed to keep any mention of Rasputin out of public life, but after his death allegations, innuendoes, and even cartoons appeared in the press, while Guchkov denounced Rasputin from the rostrum of the Duma. With uncharacteristic discretion, Rasputin fled St Petersburg for his Siberian village; on learning of his departure, the furious tsarina urged Nicholas to abolish the Duma. Guchkov's speech probably contributed to the anti-Octobrist campaign that was mounted by the clergy and encouraged by the Holy Synod during the elections held in 1912 for the Fourth Duma. Inevitably, the Rasputin scandal cast a pall over celebrations planned for the tercentenary of the Romanov dynasty in 1913.

The tsar always welcomed those who blamed Russia's misfortunes on the evil intentions of Jewish financiers, intellectuals, and revolutionaries. Some thought that the government itself deliberately encouraged, or turned a blind eye to, antisemitic outbursts. For example, Plehve himself was accused of fomenting the terrible pogrom in Kishinev in 1903, when mob violence was fuelled by rumours of a Jewish 'ritual murder'. More pogroms occurred in 1905. Although the October Manifesto implied that the innumerable restrictions on Jews would be lifted, Stolypin's tentative efforts in this direction were blocked by the tsar, who proudly wore the badge of the fanatically antisemitic Union of the Russian People. In 1913, ritual murder allegations surfaced again in Kiev when a Jew, Mendel Beilis, was tried for killing a Christian boy. Despite evidence that the crime had been committed by a local gang, the full weight of the tsarist regime – personified in this case by the Minister of Justice, Ivan Shcheglovitov – was directed at trying to prove the charges against Beilis. Russian antisemites, unconcerned that the case discredited the regime both at home and abroad, claimed partial vindication when the jury, after acquitting Beilis, nevertheless found that a ritual murder had indeed been committed by persons unknown [57, 93].

'GREAT RUSSIA': HOPES AND FEARS

A remarkable development in these last remaining years of peace was the emergence in Moscow of a new political force that rejected the traditions and outlook of both the tsarist regime and the radical intelligentsia. The 1905 Revolution had frightened most Russian businessmen into supporting the Octobrists, but a group of young liberal entrepreneurs headed by the brothers Paul and Vladimir Riabushinskii took a different course. Muscovites and mostly Old Believers, members of the 'Riabushinskii circle' shared neither the statist outlook of the St Petersburg industrialists nor the cosmopolitan materialism of the intelligentsia. Beginning in 1909, they met repeatedly with Struve and the *Landmarks* contributors, in the hope of forging a new coalition of liberal nationalists that would provide dynamic, practical and informed leadership for a rejuvenated and entrepreneurial 'Great Russia'. In 1912, they formed the Progressist Party, which elected more than forty deputies to the Fourth Duma. Their vision of the Russian future blended capitalism and neo-Slavophilism: like Shipov, they believed in the primacy of morality and in 'a religious and nationalist ethos unique to Russia' [116 *p. 48*].

Visions of a new era of industrial peace and prosperity were rudely shattered by a fresh wave of labour protest that began in April, 1912, when hundreds of striking workers were shot by soldiers in the Lena valley goldfields of eastern Siberia. When news of the massacre reached the capital, there was an explosion of protest in the factories and on the streets, as well as an outcry in the Duma and the press. Within days, the protest had spread from St Petersburg throughout the country; within a month, the number of striking workers reached almost half a million, a figure reminiscent of the turmoil of 1905–06. Faced with this renewed labour militancy, liberals and conservatives quickly convinced themselves that it could easily get out of control. Many Kadets were in despair, fearing that the growing violence could exceed that of 1905. Guchkov alarmed his fellow Octobrists by warning that unless the impending revolutionary outbreak were averted, their own heads would be among the first to roll [*Doc. 15*]. Strikes continued throughout 1913, and during the first six months of 1914 more than a million workers went on strike, with political as well as economic issues figuring among their demands.

Was this escalating labour militancy evidence of mounting social instability in urban Russia? [47]. Had it not been for the outbreak of war, might the tsarist regime have collapsed in late 1914, rather than early 1917? These questions have been debated at length by historians of Russia, most of whom would now agree that the revival of militancy, while undeniably important, was scarcely the beginning of an organized revolutionary effort. It demonstrated beyond question that the regime was incapable of devising and pursuing an imaginative and flexible labour policy [67]. In addition, it furnished dramatic evidence of the short-sightedness of employers, and of the police and military officials who reinforced their authority. Yet in St Petersburg especially, the degree of unrest was neither uniform nor seriously revolutionary: Western historians have disproven earlier Soviet claims that the militancy was planned or directed by the Bolsheviks; nor, for that matter, was it the work of other socialist parties [69]. The typical prewar militant in the Imperial capital was likely to be a skilled metalworker who distrusted intelligentsia organizers as much as he despised policemen and factory inspectors. Nevertheless, the Bolsheviks, with their maximalist programme, appeared closer to the militant mood of Russian workers than did the Mensheviks or the SRs.

6 'FATEFUL YEARS', 1914–17

In the summer of 1914, perceived threats to Russia's great power status led a reluctant but defiant Nicholas II into war with Germany and Austria-Hungary. By no means indifferent to human suffering, the tsar was understandably averse to forcing upon his subjects the incalculable hardships of war – hardships that were likely to be all the greater, his advisers warned, because at that moment Russian preparations for a major European war were not yet complete. In the wake of Japan's stunning victories, plans had been made to rebuild the navy and reorganize the army, but the planners believed that another war was unlikely before 1916 at the earliest. When worsening international tensions in 1912–13 proved the flimsiness of that assumption, Russians were forced to weigh the costs of preserving peace against the risks of making war. One highly-placed bureaucrat, Peter Durnovo, endeavoured – prophetically, it soon appeared – to persuade the tsar that there was everything to lose and nothing to gain from a war between Russia and Germany [61]. However, he spoke for a very small minority; most of the tsar's ministers and senior officials had come to believe that an expansionist and adventurist Germany was now the principal threat to the peace of Europe and the survival of the Russian Empire. Durnovo's conviction that war would inevitably engulf Russia in revolution was, however, shared by Lenin, who wrote (January 1913) that he doubted whether the tsar and the Austrian Emperor would ever do such a favour for the revolutionary cause in eastern Europe [41].

The international crisis that led to war was touched off by a Serbian terrorist who assassinated the heir to the Austrian throne, Crown Prince Franz Ferdinand, in the Bosnian city of Sarajevo on 15/28 June 1914. Austria had occupied the former Ottoman provinces of Bosnia and Herzegovina since 1878, a situation that rankled Serbs who hoped that their country would become the principal beneficiary of the decline of the Ottoman power in the Balkans. The Austrian occupation was part of an international agreement imposed on Russia decades earlier by other European powers who feared the political consequences of Russian military success against the Turks. This diplomatic defeat left Russian nationalists with feelings of betrayal and humiliation, wounds that were not only reopened but aggravated when their armies and fleets were so resoundingly defeated by the Japanese, whom they had mistakenly thought to be a lesser foe. Then, in 1908, Russian imperial pretensions were flouted once again by the Austrians who, with German support, took advantage of Russia's military weakness and recent civil disarray to turn their occupation of Bosnia into a formal annexation, internationally recognized by the other powers. In the Duma, the Octobrist leader Guchkov gave vent to the frustration of those who felt that Russia's interests had been disregarded yet again: even if war was at that moment out of the question, he still regretted Russia's failure to secure some compensatory advantage from the situation. This legacy of repeated humiliations extending over more than three decades played an important part in shaping Russia's response to the unfolding crisis in July 1914.

That response was directed by the tsar himself, who genuinely hoped to avoid war but who also refused to be bullied into submission. This position was soon made untenable by the behaviour of the German and Austro-Hungarian governments. The latter used the assassination of Franz Ferdinand as a pretext for making impossible demands upon the Serbs, thereby provoking a Russian declaration of support for their 'Slavic brothers' whose very survival as a nation-state now seemed in jeopardy. Austria-Hungary, aware of the Russian position but fortified by the open support of Germany, broke off diplomatic relations with Serbia and on 15/28 July declared war, launching an immediate attack on the Serbian capital, Belgrade. Russia, with the strong support of her ally, France, and the noticeably less enthusiastic support of Great Britain, began to mobilize selected military and naval units. On 17/30 July, both Russia and Austria-Hungary announced general mobilization, but Germany immediately sent Russia an ultimatum threatening war unless Russia backed down. This the tsar refused to do, and when the ultimatum expired Germany declared war on Russia, followed quickly by Austria-Hungary. Germany also declared war on France and when the immediate German offensive violated Belgian neutrality, Great Britain declared war on Germany. The Great War had begun.

The day before mobilization was announced, the tsar approved a new Statute on the Field Administration of the Army in Wartime; it gave the commander-in-chief and his staff effective control over both military operations and civil government throughout the entire war zone, including not only the front itself but the adjacent areas of the rear. Although it would take several months for the law's full implications to become apparent, Nicholas had, at the stroke of a pen, drastically reduced the authority and jurisdiction of his own ministers, who were soon dismayed to discover how little influence they wielded in wartime Russia. With hostilities imminent, the tsar's first thought was that he should become commander-in-chief, in order to put himself at the head of the entire war effort, but within days advisers prevailed on him not to take such a risk with his person and the fortunes of the dynasty. Consequently, on 19 July the tsar appointed his uncle, Grand Duke Nicholas, commander-in-chief and director of military operations at field headquarters (*Stavka**). The Field Administration Statute assigned matters of supply and logistics to the War Ministry in St Petersburg, a sensible enough plan in theory, but it ignored the fact that War Minister Sukhomlinov and the new commander-in-chief were old opponents who were utterly incapable of co-operating with one another. Typically, the tsar appears to have been oblivious to the potentially chaotic situation that he had helped to create.

For Nicholas, the prospect of suffering was partially offset by the solemnity of the moment: he was extraordinarily moved when thousands of his subjects greeted his appearance on the Winter Palace balcony by kneeling and singing 'God Save the Tsar'. Monarchists immediately took heart, easily convincing themselves that the huge national effort demanded by the war would overcome the social tensions and political animosities of the past two decades [Doc. 16]. When Nicholas and Alexandra visited Moscow, they encountered patriotic demonstrations every bit as enthusiastic as those in St Petersburg, an experience which led Nicholas to conclude that all his subjects were prepared to bury their differences for the duration of the war, following the example of the Duma deputies who had already promised to put the national interest ahead of any party political considerations.

The crucial question, however, was whether this outburst of civilian patriotism could be channelled and institutionalized in ways that were both militarily useful and politically innocuous. Learning from the example of Japan in 1904–1905, other belligerent powers found that encouraging their national Red Cross societies not only assisted the army's fighting capacity but also provided a necessary and carefully regulated outlet for patriotic enthusiasm. The Russian Red Cross society might have played such a role – its charitable and relief work over several decades had created a favourable popular image – but only if the regime could readily welcome popular support and encourage the spontaneous activity of enthusiastic volunteers. However, all the traditions of Russian bureaucracy, both military and civil, ran in the opposite direction; patriotic civilians soon found that their motives were suspect, their energy resented, and their enthusiasm treated as interference. Although Empress Alexandra and her daughters, like other royal ladies across Europe, dutifully set a good example by rolling bandages and nursing the wounded, their labours were largely in vain: where in other countries wartime voluntary work became a source of strength and national unity, in Russia it became a focus for political tension and divisiveness.

THE POLITICAL ECONOMY OF WAR

The first lesson that Russians learned in the battlefields of Poland and East Prussia was that German firepower was truly staggering, far beyond anything anticipated by the planners or discerned by military intelligence [107]. Consequently, the army's medical services were immediately overwhelmed by the sheer number of wounded and maimed soldiers, many of whom were simply loaded into straw-filled freight cars and abruptly despatched to the rear. When the first of these hastily improvised evacuation trains arrived in Moscow, where no appropriate preparations had been made, sensitive observers quickly grasped both the scale of the disaster at the front and the potential for utter chaos in the rear [11]. Within days, the Moscow provincial zemstvo asked the tsar to sanction the formation of an All-Russian Union of Zemstvos, a temporary national organization that would co-ordinate medical and other assistance to the army; municipal leaders quickly followed suit by proposing the creation of a Union of Towns. Nicholas II, buoyed up by the burgeoning patriotic unity, quickly replied with a telegram that welcomed these initiatives. His hasty, positive response shocked conservative officials who were dismayed that the wartime crisis had so easily enabled these groups to escape the legal restrictions normally imposed on their activities.

As if to demonstrate that the imperial family could save the army from further debacles, Nicholas announced in early September that a newly created military unit dealing with the care and transport of the wounded would be headed by his cousin, Prince Alexander Oldenburg, a respected philanthropist. In this new position as head of the Sanitary and Evacuation Section, Oldenburg became in effect a dictator, exempt from all military and civil control except that of the commander-in chief. His first task was to co-ordinate relations between the military and the two new voluntary organizations which, the tsar had stipulated, ought to work as auxiliaries to the Russian Red Cross. This goal Oldenburg sought to achieve by drawing a demarcation line from Moscow to Kharkov in the Ukraine: all areas west of this line were to be controlled by the army and the Red Cross, while the eastern, rear areas would fall to the voluntary organizations. The prince suspected the motives of those active in the zemstvo and municipal unions; many of their leaders had connections with the Kadets, Progressives, and Octobrists, and he feared that they wanted to interfere in the war effort mainly to embarrass the government. Hence his desire to keep them at a distance. In practice, however, the 'Oldenburg line' could not be maintained because hard pressed corps commanders sought help wherever they could get it: General Brusilov, for example, asked the Zemstvo Union to send medical teams and field hospitals to his army in Galicia [54].

Both internal and external factors impelled the voluntary organizations to expand their personnel and activity. Soon they faced the threat of epidemic disease, which increased substantially when the authorities decided to clear all operational areas of so-called 'unreliable' elements among the civilian population. These orders fell with particular severity upon the Jews [*Doc. 17*], but they were by no means alone; in the west, Germans, Latvians and Poles also found themselves summarily evicted from their homes, as did Turks, Greeks and Armenians in the Caucasus. These enforced removals clogged the roads and railways of European Russia with refugees, impairing both the evacuation of wounded and the transport of military personnel and supplies, and helping to spread infectious diseases, especially typhus, which reached epidemic proportions by the early summer of 1915. Not surprisingly, the technical and professional bureaux of the Unions developed their own internal dynamics, partially because they had been staffed in haste with individuals whose dislike for the tsarist regime had earlier cost them professional positions, if not during the 'zemstvo reaction' of 1906–1907, then during Kasso's purge of the universities, and who, it soon emerged, were considerably more radical than the liberals who were the nominal leaders of the voluntary organizations. With trains, hospitals, factories and equipment under their control, the technical and professional staff soon developed bolder agendas that affected relations with the government while producing tensions within the Unions themselves [44].

From the first days of the war, the army found itself continually short of shells and ammunition. By the spring of 1915, a full-scale 'munitions crisis' erupted, resulting in the creation of a third voluntary organization. The shortage was not simply the result of poor planning, but a consequence of the close ties between the Ministry of War and its traditional suppliers in Petrograd (the more Russian-sounding wartime name for St Petersburg). Although industrial enterprises in Moscow or the Urals might easily have been able to fulfil orders and avert the shortage, the Ministry preferred to order abroad rather than undermine the dominant position of the 'military-industrial complex' in Petrograd [102]. The shortage became a political issue when Rodzianko, President of the Fourth Duma, made a much-publicized visit to the front during the retreat from Galicia in the spring of 1915. Two responses ensued. Yielding to pleas from Rodzianko, who was tacitly supported by the commander-in-chief, Nicholas created a Special Council on Defence, but this body was quickly seized on by the Petrograd industrialists as a way of maintaining their unofficial monopoly on defence contracts. Meanwhile, a national congress of Russian industrialists, dominated by Moscow manufacturers, voted to create War Industries Committees throughout the country, ostensibly to rally the patriotic support of employers and workers in order to avert the munitions shortage. More than patriotism was at work here, however, for these would-be saviours of Russia were closely connected to the Riabushinskii circle and the Progressist Party; almost certainly they hoped to use the war as a means of ensuring that Moscow replaced Petrograd as the leading force in the future industrial development of the country [102]. It was no accident that they asked the former Octobrist leader Guchkov, himself the scion of a well-known Moscow business family, to direct the formation of the War Industries Committees.

SUMMER 1915: CRISIS ON TWO FRONTS

The Moscow industrialists were not alone in their desire to use the war to advance their own objectives: news of the worsening military situation led the Duma deputies to put aside their earlier pledge of support and seek opportunities to criticize the regime's conduct of the war. The government had permitted a three-day session in January, 1915, but only on the condition that the Duma do nothing except approve budget estimates; by May, deputies eager to reconvene were furious at the government's continuing refusal to provide them with a platform. Duma President Rodzianko, anxious to revive the flagging spirit of national unity, convinced the tsar not only to dismiss the now discredited War Minister Sukhomlinov and three other ministers whose enthusiasm for the war had been questioned, but also to agree to a summer session of the Duma. Meanwhile, leading moderates in the Duma began trying to create an inter-party alliance so that they could present a united front to the government when the session began on 19 July.

The result was that a working coalition of Kadets, Octobrists and Centrists now called for the formation of a 'ministry of confidence', a deliberately more temperate demand than the leftists' adamant insistence on a ministry responsible to the Duma. For a time, relations appeared cordial: the new War Minister, General Polivanov, invited Duma representatives to join the new Council on Defence, while the deputies vented their hostility on the disgraced Sukhomlinov, whose association with a German spy led to his impeachment for high treason. A month later, the moderates – now calling themselves the Progressive Bloc – published their demands, the main thrust of which was that a new government enjoying the confidence of the country should be formed and immediately begin carrying out an agreed legislative programme [*Doc. 18*]. Several of the tsar's ministers were favourably disposed towards the Bloc, but formal negotiations could not begin without the tsar's approval.

The tsar, meanwhile, had hit upon his own solution to Russia's military reverses: he would himself take command at the front. Both Grand Duke Nicholas and his Chief of Staff, General Ianushkevich, were to be relieved of their posts. Nicholas was certain that the physical presence of their tsar would rally the spirits of ordinary Russian soldiers and put new life into Stavka. When on 6 August the incredulous ministers were told of his plans, all – except their Chairman, the doddering but loyal Goremykin – thought it a recipe for both military and political disaster. After repeated attempts to dissuade him from this course failed, eight of them formally requested that the tsar relieve them of their positions, but Nicholas left for the front without replying. Several ministers, aware of growing support in Moscow and among Russian industrialists for the demands of the Progressive Bloc, began discussions with Bloc representatives, but their attempts at bridge-building were forestalled by the tsar, who sent orders from Stavka for the Duma to be prorogued immediately; all his ministers were to remain at their posts until further notice. This message effectively scotched further negotiations with the Bloc [77].

After the 1917 revolution, liberal historians armed with hindsight condemned Nicholas' behaviour, faulting him not only for preventing an agreement with the Duma moderates, but also for leaving the government of the country in the hands of the empress and her confidante Rasputin, and thereby aggravating fears that pro-German 'dark forces' were ruling unchallenged in Petrograd [75]. Such a harsh judgement is no longer acceptable. For one thing, the Bloc's programme papered over significant differences of opinion that might well have destroyed its momentary unity. Moreover, the alarmist ministers were wrong in their predictions of military and political disaster; indeed, on both scores 1916 would prove a considerably better year for the tsarist regime [60]. Finally, civil government suffered not so much from the haphazard and petty interference of Rasputin as from the general paralysis brought on by the exigencies of war. With so much of the country already under military rule, the tsar's increasingly impotent ministers sought to prevent the voluntary organizations from becoming shadow governments by stonewalling their requests for state subsidies; some even feared lest the War Industries Committees be used to plot the overthrow of the government, but in 1915 such fears were groundless: Guchkov was intent on avoiding, not fomenting, a revolution.

DANGEROUS GAMES

Surprisingly dangerous games were played in wartime Russia. The most risky of these involved a calculated attempt by Russian industrialists and their political allies to stop workers from disrupting war production, ostensibly by giving them a stake in the war and thus persuading them to postpone industrial conflict and political struggles until the war's end. Clearly this attempt was prompted by rising labour tensions and strikes in the spring and summer of 1915 in Moscow, and in the mines and metalworks of the crucially important Donbass region. To avert further disruption, Guchkov, assisted by Paul Riabushinskii and Alexander Konovalov (both Moscow textile manufacturers) hastily devised a plan to create elected workers' groups within the War Industries Committees. The government, too timid to squash the idea immediately, reluctantly agreed, its unexpected decision forcing the left-wing parties to decide whether or not to participate in the elections. Advocates of a complete boycott taunted their opponents with the charge that they were being duped, but those who argued for participation saw the scheme as a chance to organize legally and fight against the ruthless exploitation of workers by war profiteers.

At this point the risks became apparent. Confronted by the hostility or scepticism of Petrograd bureaucrats and bankers, the organizers of the scheme responded by enthusiastically touting its merits. Konovalov's injudicious boast that he had created a bulwark against industrial anarchy soon forced the elected workers' representatives to distance themselves from the bosses by claiming complete autonomy from their parent organization, the Central War Industries Committee. He and his colleagues were unable to prevent this radical shift, dramatized when a congress of workers' representatives called in February, 1916, for the creation of a government responsible to the Duma, the convening of a congress of all Russian workers, and the introduction of a minimum wage [102]. At this juncture, Konovalov had to force concessions from the government, or else he would find himself holding a tiger by the tail.

Yet in the spring and summer of 1916 such concessions were most unlikely. From the government's point of view, both the military and the political situation had altered substantially for the better since the previous year. The retreat had been stopped without the loss of Kiev, a matter of considerable symbolic importance, and the supply situation was much improved. In the summer, General Brusilov's army launched a brilliantly successful offensive on the southwestern front, capturing numerous prisoners, both German and Austrian. The military turnaround had been made possible largely by War Minister Polivanov, whom knowledgeable observers considered an outstanding organizer of personnel, training, supplies, and equipment. Nevertheless, in March, 1916, Polivanov was brusquely dismissed by Nicholas II, allegedly because his supervision of the War Industries Committees had been 'insufficiently authoritative' [75 p. 327]. His departure signalled the beginning of a concerted campaign, orchestrated in the spring and summer of 1916 by a revived Council of Ministers, to intimidate and discredit the voluntary organizations, particularly the War Industries Committees. For example, the new Minister of Trade and Industry, Prince Vsevolod Shakhovskoi, sought to weaken their hold on coal and oil production by creating state monopolies that would allow the government, not the producers, to set prices. In such a changed atmosphere there was no likelihood whatever that the far-reaching demands of the workers' groups would be accepted, and within those organizations dissatisfaction mounted as fruitless months passed with no sign of concessions from the government. Stung by criticisms from Martov and the Mensheviks, the workers' groups decided in November, 1916, to try to direct the strike movement in St Petersburg towards the overthrow of the tsarist regime and the creation of a revolutionary government [102].

This overt change of course soon produced unexpected responses elsewhere. Guchkov decided that his last resort, a palace revolution against Nicholas II, was the only hope of averting the revolution that he now believed to be inevitable. He had reluctantly concluded that the evolutionary, reformist course being followed by the Duma moderates – a course he himself had followed for many years – was ultimately futile in a Russia where official intransigence both ignored and fuelled popular revolutionary attitudes. Invited to attend a secret meeting of Duma leaders called in September, 1916, to discuss the worsening political situation, he was both dismayed by their persistent belief that Nicholas would eventually give in to the demand for a 'ministry of confidence', and appalled at their naive assumption that if a revolution came, they would naturally be asked to direct it.

Convinced that anarchy could be forestalled only by forcing the tsar to abdicate the throne in favour of his son Alexis, with Grand Duke Michael acting as regent, Guchkov and two associates worked out a plan to capture the emperor and force him to sign an abdication decree. Planning their *coup* for March, 1917, the conspirators began attracting support among army officers, whose assistance would be crucial to its success. Guchkov had no intention of turning the government of Russia over to the leaders of the Progressive Bloc, whom he thought lacking in courage; instead, he planned a reformed ministry that would include himself and his associates, as well as a handful of the tsar's most able and sympathetic ministers, notably Agriculture Minister Alexis Krivoshein and Foreign Minister Sergei Sazonov.

Another, pathetically misguided, attempt to avert revolution was the murder of Rasputin in December, 1916, by three conspirators from the social and political right wing. In this sordid enterprise a demagogue orator from the Union of the Russian People, a naively romantic aristocrat, and an impetuous young member of the Imperial family joined forces, having convinced themselves that by eliminating Rasputin they would save the empress from further disgrace, the dynasty from certain collapse, and Holy Russia from corrupting immorality. Despite the formidable efforts required to dispatch the powerful Siberian, the conspirators attained none of their goals; instead they earned the antipathy of the empress, who with characteristic logic held Rasputin's critics equally responsible for his death.

INTO THE STREETS: THE END OF THE MONARCHY

By late 1916, war had taken a severe toll on the economy of Russia. The railway system, much of it built to serve the grain export trade of the Black Sea ports, proved itself both inadequate and inappropriate for meeting the needs of war on a front that stretched from the Baltic to the Carpathians and into Asia Minor. To offset the expenses of war the government printed more and more paper money, and the resulting inflation created a steadily widening gap between the cost of basic necessities and the wages that ordinary Russians were paid, be they industrial workers, shop assistants, or government clerks. Moreover, in the black-earth provinces of southern Russia, peasants who resented the fixed prices set by army requisitions preferred to hold onto surplus grain rather than sell it at prices that seemed to lag behind rising costs. In these circumstances, it became increasingly difficult to provide the urban centres of northern Russia with sufficient food. Hardship was felt particularly keenly in Petrograd, where a police report in October, 1916, warned authorities that the 'half-starved existence' of the masses had made them 'ready for the most wild excesses on the first suitable or unsuitable occasion' [60 *p. 219*]. For those who daily faced the misery of urban life, the fact that several notoriously luxurious restaurants continued to flourish throughout the war only sharpened the growing resentment against wealth and privilege, a bitterness directed especially against those reaping huge profits from war contracts.

Against this backdrop of frustration, the workers' representatives decided to push the current wave of strikes beyond economic grievances and into the realm of political action. Plans were laid for country-wide one-day strikes on 9 January 1917, to commemorate the anniversary of Bloody Sunday, but these were disrupted when police arrested many of those involved. The few who escaped the crackdown decided to shift their focus to the Duma, now due to meet on 14 February, in the hope that a non-violent demonstration of popular support for an end to tsarism would move the Progressive Bloc considerably to the left. This proved to be a whopping miscalculation: faced with thousands of striking workers and dozens of closed factories, the moderates' response was anything but sympathetic. All of them sought to pre-empt revolutionary action by the aroused urban population, Guchkov by accelerating his plans for a coup, Miliukov by insisting on a 'legal' transfer of power from the tsar to himself, and Rodzianko by trying to persuade the tsar to appoint him head of a 'ministry of confidence' [77].

The next crisis caught everyone off guard. On 20 February, flour and bread rationing were introduced in Moscow, and rumours of impending starvation soon flew through Petrograd. Three days later, the huge Putilov munitions works locked out 40,000 workers, providing the motivation for a sympathetic general strike on 24 February, which was also International Women's Day. As the demonstrations grew larger, they were joined by mutinous soldiers from the Petrograd garrison. At Stavka, the tsar was kept apprised of the situation in Petrograd by the military governor and the police; he also received a sheaf of telegrams from the now panicky Rodzianko, who warned that the monarchy would collapse unless concessions were made immediately. Nicholas responded by proroguing the Duma and ordering measures for the restoration of order, but by then it was too late. When insurgent soldiers and self-declared revolutionary guards arrived in the building where the Duma met, even diehard monarchists like Rodzianko were forced to become reluctant revolutionaries in a desperate attempt to keep power from falling into the hands of the newly-formed Petrograd Soviet [Council] of Workers' (and soon Soldiers') Deputies.

The tsar's abdication was now unpreventable, although ironically it was Nicholas II's most vocal critics who tried their best to ensure that the monarchy itself survived. Abandoning his planned *coup*, Guchkov joined his fellow industrialists in calling for Grand Duke Michael to be named regent immediately, so that a new government could order an end to the strikes and get on with the war. Miliukov, whom conservatives had long suspected of closet republicanism, emerged in 1917 as the monarchy's last outspoken defender; he feared that in the face of mass pressure any provisional government would collapse without the symbolic legitimacy derived from the continuation of the monarchy. Meanwhile Nicholas, still believing that disaster could be averted, set out for Petrograd, but his train was halted at Pskov, where emissaries from the hastily created 'Provisional Committee of the Duma' brought him a draft abdication decree. By now fresh assessments of the political situation had reached him, not only from Rodzianko but also from most of his top-ranking military officers, all of whom agreed on the need for a dramatic gesture to halt the apparent collapse of military and civil authority. After much soul-searching, he agreed to abdicate, but not, as requested, in favour of his sickly heir Alexis; instead he passed the crown directly to Grand Duke Michael, a decision that made the task of saving the dynasty even more difficult. One can imagine the exasperation and despair of the emissaries, both of whom were monarchists, when the tsar, after signing the decree, asked '... in a curiously simple way: "Do you think it might have been avoided?" ' [14 *p. 277*].

PART THREE: ASSESSMENT

7 LATE IMPERIAL RUSSIA AND THE HISTORIANS

Could Imperial Russia have avoided the fate that befell it in 1917? For half a century after its collapse, historians in the English-speaking world were certain that the answer to this question was a resounding 'yes'. This was mainly because their perceptions of what had happened in Russia were moulded by the legion of former Kadets and Octobrists who fled the country when it became clear that the Civil War would end in victory for the Bolsheviks. In speeches, lectures, newspaper articles and memoirs, these embittered emigrés blamed Nicholas II personally, and the tsarist regime generally, for their own (by now painfully obvious) inability to harness the revolutionary energy that swept across Russia in the months following the tsar's abdication. British and American historians soon joined in the exiles' lament for the fate of Russian liberalism, which was based on a series of 'if onlys': if only the tsar had authorized negotiations with the Progressive Bloc in 1915; if only he had agreed to Rodzianko's pleas for a 'ministry of confidence'; if only the regime had made a sincere effort to work with the Duma; if only the tsar had not reneged on the letter and spirit of the October Manifesto. In this version of events, Nicholas II had dozens of opportunities to prevent the disaster of revolution, but because of his own ignorance, naiveté, and obstinacy he let every one of them slip through his hands. Worse still, so the story went, he allowed himself to be duped by his wife into distrusting the integrity of the patriotic Duma leaders and industrialists whose first priority was to win the war against Germany.

Blaming the tsar for the outcome of 1917 enabled the emigres and the historians to avoid asking questions about the degree of popular support for the Duma or the programme of Russian liberalism. Yet such questions cannot be avoided. On the eve of the First World War, Guchkov himself had warned that a popular revolution would surely be directed against the propertied classes, while Durnovo had predicted that the liberals' inability to control the masses would lead to political anarchy and the destruction of private property and social privilege. These frank evaluations of the weakness of popular support for what liberals called 'the rule of law' made nonsense of later attempts to put all the blame for Lenin's success on the failings of the last tsar. Yet despite this glaring contradiction, the interpretive framework established in the twenties survived for many decades. This is largely attributable to the exigencies of the Cold War. In the hands of those who preached the values of liberal capitalism, history was a weapon to be used to explain why Russia's 'natural' evolution had been frustrated, first by tsarist bureaucrats and then by a Bolshevik conspiracy. In the Soviet Union, meanwhile, students were taught that the so-called liberals of the prerevolutionary period used constitutional doctrines and patriotic slogans to disguise their plans for the development of imperialist capitalism. In such a highly charged atmosphere, withholding (or, in Soviet Russia, conferring) political legitimacy was a much higher priority than serious historical investigation. Fifty years after the 1917 Revolution, an anniversary colloquium of British and American scholars and diplomats resoundingly endorsed all the old liberal pieties [79].

In the last four decades, however, this edifice has crumbled into ruins, and the historical landscape of late Imperial Russia has been dramatically transformed. The ancient litany of 'if onlys' was swept aside by scholars who boldly questioned liberal verities about the decisive influence of the First World War, the eventual triumph of liberal democracy in village Russia, and the lack of popular support for Lenin's seizure of power [47, 84, 95]. Bored by the old preoccupation with bureaucratic opposition to constitutionalism, a new generation of historians intent on writing 'history from below' set out to recover the travails and identify the aspirations of the lower classes. The result was a torrent of books on soldiers, peasants, and especially workers – factory workers, urban workers, migrant workers, radical workers, railway workers, women workers – that soon provided an alternative social history capable of displacing the older political history of revolutionary Russia [1, 108]. Two main themes dominated this new work: not only was the collapse of Imperial Russia unavoidable because of the gulf that separated the elite from the masses, but the social tensions of 1917 were found to be so well established before 1914 that they were merely aggravated – certainly not caused – by three years of war. Eventually, in the mid-1980s, the last remaining pillars of the old liberal interpretation were dismantled when one revisionist scholar persuasively argued that the patriotic industrialists of wartime Russia were really liberal imperialists motivated by capitalist greed, while another questioned the standard clichés about the indecisiveness of the tsar and the malevolence of his 'reactionary' advisers [60, 102]. Late Imperial Russia was rapidly becoming a far more complex, and therefore far more exciting and challenging, historical terrain.

In the last two decades the outpouring of new work, which began even before the collapse of the Soviet Union transformed archival access, has only added to the richness of the subject. While generalizations are risky, much of it appears to confirm the verdict reached in 1909 by the contributors to the *Vekhi* symposium: that by the beginning of this century, both the tsarist regime and the Russian intelligentsia were fossilized relics of the past, incapable of responding constructively to the challenges posed by capitalist industrialization and the concomitant social transformation of the empire. The autocracy's inability to devise a workable system of industrial relations may well have been symptomatic of a deeper, more fundamental conflict between the values and imperatives of capitalism and those of the tsarist regime [67]. Those bureaucrats who understood the need for reform continually ran up against a tsar determined to uphold the ideology of autocracy and the privileges of the landed nobility [46, 64, 113]. Although Nicholas II's most empathetic biographer now sees firmness where so many others saw malleability, the tsar's 'unshakable will' sometimes led him to take positions that were in the end self-defeating. One example is his determination to protect his family from criticism. Noting his outrage when Duma orators attacked the retrograde influence of the Grand Dukes in military matters, for example, a recent study concludes that 'most of the Romanovs never grasped the professional needs of the institution that legitimized and maintained their power' [106 *p. 288*].

If the tsarist regime appeared to lose its footing after the turn of the century, members of the intelligentsia were also caught unawares by increasing evidence that the unfolding Russian future might conform neither to their ideological expectations nor to their cultural preferences. If the years before 1905 were punctuated by unpleasant reminders of the distance that separated radical intellectuals from politically aware workers, the rural violence of 1905–06 demonstrated the continuing gulf between the hungry and poverty-stricken peasants of Russia and the empire's privileged elites, of which the intelligentsia, however reluctantly, were an obvious and inescapable part. Even more disconcerting, perhaps, was the uncomfortable realization that the country's increasing literacy would not necessarily promote, let alone guarantee, the cultural hegemony of the intelligentsia.

In the last decades of tsarist rule, a new mass reading public developed an appetite for books and newspapers that was soon satisfied by astute and imaginative publishers who, by systematically encouraging the growth of an independent public opinion, created a public space that was beyond the control of either the regime or the intelligentsia [24, 70]. However, the favourite subjects of popular readers – adventure stories with a jingoist or nationalist twist, for example – predictably evoked lofty disdain from members of the intelligentsia who believed that only they should decide what sort of literature would promote the ethical development of the Russian people, a view shared, ironically, by those who staffed the regime's increasingly embattled censorship offices. Not all of these new readers were city-dwellers. Rural literacy was also growing, in part because peasants wanted to read and count, if only to protect themselves against deception or exploitation; in part because of the great expansion of rural elementary schools, many of them run by the zemstvos [31]. Inevitably, both the traditional isolation of the Russian village and its suspicion of outsiders were affected by the growth of literacy, the pace of industrialization, and the increasing frequency of contacts between rural and urban areas, changes which in 1905–07 transformed rural schoolteachers from objects of universal contempt into respected and influential rural activists [99]. The huge psychological distance which village Russia would need to travel in order to become part of an integrated national community has been forcefully underlined by scholars who have analysed popular ideas about crime, punishment, justice and order within rural communities [35].

As attention has shifted away from conflict between the tsarist regime and the political intelligentsia, historians have naturally extended their field of vision to include not only St Petersburg, but all of urban Russia; and not only the elites, but also the denizens of low life, whose presence on the streets so disconcerted their fellow urban dwellers [23]. Both the uniquely Russian and the universal aspects of urbanization have been explored in separate studies of Moscow, Kiev, and Odessa [49, 51, 112]. Whether the cities of late Imperial Russia ought to be seen as backward and undeveloped places experiencing a crisis of urban modernization, or as vibrant centres characterized by social mobility and the remarkable survival skills of their inhabitants has been the subject of considerable controversy [25, 105]. City-dwelling businessmen have also come under special scrutiny from those searching for evidence of the development of a 'bourgeois consciousness' in Russia [29]. At least until 1905, the merchants of Moscow do not appear to have been the dynamic innovators and risk-takers that one expects in an entrepreneurial culture [74, 96]. Even after this relatively late political awakening, social fragmentation and geographic separation among Russian businessmen arguably prevented the emergence of a homogeneous Russian bourgeoisie [89]. One undoubted consequence of this vacuum was the socially skewed development of liberalism, which in Russia remained chiefly a creation of the intelligentsia and of those newly important professional groups such as professors, physicians and engineers, that have been called 'Russia's missing middle class' [19, 56].

Unquestionably, this interest in 'educated society and the quest for public identity' [29] has produced a more subtle and nuanced understanding of the interactions between the tsarist regime and Russian society; of the plight and aspirations of the 'educated middle' including, but not limited to, the nascent bourgeoisie; of the important roles played by women, both inside the factory and inside the family; and a new appreciation of the unusual opportunities for social and political change that were created, postponed, or destroyed by Russia's participation in the First World War. Nevertheless, there are already clear indications that historians, ever restless, are developing new preoccupations. One likely to prove especially fruitful is a new concern with the peoples of the empire's borderlands, particularly the nomadic and semi-nomadic Islamic peoples of Turkestan. This recent interest in 'Russia's Orient' is partially a response to provocative recent analyses of orientalism and imperialism, and partially a product of attempts to understand the fluid situation in post-Soviet Central Asia. It has already shown itself likely to open up lines of inquiry that were hitherto literally inconceivable. An example is the provocative suggestion that historians should now explore, from a comparative approach, the dilemmas that the tsarist regime faced in creating a conception of citizenship that would accommodate both the nomadic population of the empire and the peasantry of the Russian countryside [119]. Whatever may come from pursuing such intriguing agendas, one can only delight in this evidence of fresh interest in late Imperial Russia as a field of historical inquiry. Its continued vibrancy in the English-speaking world is all the more important and necessary given the regrettable haste with which contemporary Russians are repudiating their revolutionary past and romanticizing the closing decades of the tsarist era.

PART FOUR: DOCUMENTS

DOCUMENT 1   RUSSIA'S FUTURE AS A EURASIAN POWER

Finance Minister Witte, sounding much like a Russian Cecil Rhodes, explains the empire's mission in Asia to Tsar Alexander III.

Standing on the confines of two such different worlds, in close contact with each of them, Russia none the less represents a world apart. Her independent place in the family of peoples and her special role in world history are determined both by her geographical position and, in particular, by the original character of her political and cultural development, a development which has been achieved through the living interaction and harmonious combination of three elements that have manifested their full creative power only in Russia. These elements are: first, Orthodoxy, preserving in purity the true spirit of Christianity, as the basis of education and upbringing; secondly, autocracy as the basis of state life; thirdly, the Russian national spirit, as the basis of the internal cohesiveness of the state, a national spirit that creates a strong inward centre, closely united yet free from nationalistic exclusiveness, possessed of a vast capacity for friendly companionship and cooperation with the most diverse races and peoples. It is on these bases that the whole edifice of Russian power has been built up, and it is therefore impossible for Russia to be fused with the West. At the same time she has long since appeared among Asiatic peoples as the bearer of the Christian ideal, striving to spread among them the principles of Christian enlightenment, not under the standard of Europeanization, but under her own special standard. In a word, in the Asiatic East Russia has long since taken upon herself the mission of cultural enlightenment in the spirit of those principles which have given a special character to her own development.

Theodore H. von Laue, [114], pp. 87–8.

DOCUMENT 2   **THE 'FEVER' FOR REFORM**

As the lay administrator of the Russian Orthodox Church and former tutor of Tsar Nicholas II, the arch-conservative Pobedonostsev did his best to thwart attempts to reform the empire's political and social structure. Here he explains why he considers the 'fever' for reform a pernicious influence.

The word reform is so often repeated that we have begun to confound it with improvement. In the popular opinion the apostles of reform are the apostles of improvement, or, as we say, progress; while on the other hand, those who question the need or utility of reform upon new principles are enemies of progress, enemies of advancement, enemies almost of good, of justice, and of civilisation. In this opinion, so widely disseminated by our publicists, there is a great error and delusion. With such errors current a common-sense judgment on any subject finds it hard to make a path through prejudices; and concrete, actual, healthy thought must surrender to abstraction and fantasy. Men of action and knowledge are forced to give place to dreamers armed with abstract ideas enveloped in loud phrases. On the other hand, he enjoys credit from the first who poses as the representative of new ideas, the advocate of reform, who carries plans in his hands for the construction of new buildings. The political profession is crowded with architects, and all who would be workmen, landlords, or tenants must needs be architects first. It is plain that with such tendencies of thought and taste an infinite field is open for all manner of charlatanry, for all the dexterity of the hypocrite, and the daring of ignorance; while practical work is hampered beyond measure when accomplished in the midst of a disposition to analysis and criticism, and subjected to the test of the general principles and phrases which obtain currency in the world. He who ought to concentrate all his attention and all his strength upon his work, and upon devising means the better to fulfil it, must constantly take into account the opinions of others, and the impression it will produce on the world and on superiors, more especially if those superiors are infected with the new ideas. Thus, on criticism and resistance to criticism, for the most part quite absurd, is wasted much force which might have accomplished great work; so much time goes in friction, in unfruitful struggle, that but little remains for real, concentrated labour. The worker is surrounded on all sides by illusory work, while the real and needed work slips from his hands and is left undone. Such a position is intolerable by good and earnest men. When concerned with life itself, with facts and living forces, they feel themselves strong; they trust in their work, and this trust gives them the power to create wonders in the actual world. But they lose heart when they deal with images, symptoms, forms, and phrases; then they have no faith, and without faith all work is fruitless. Shall we wonder then that the best workers retire, or – what is worse and what more often happens – without leaving their posts, become indifferent to their duties, fulfilling them outwardly only for the sake of influence and emolument?

Such are often the consequences of the fever for reform when it extends too far ... Meantime it is enough to pass through the streets of cities, great or small, to see at every step the ameliorations we need. Everywhere round lie formless masses of abandoned work, forsaken institutions, and ruined temples. There are schools where the teachers have forsaken the pupils to compose papers on methods of instruction, or wordy discourses for public meetings; colleges where, under the externals of education, nothing is learnt, and the bewildered teachers, in the confusion of orders and instructions, know not what to teach; there are hospitals where the afflicted fear to go because of the cold, the hunger, and the disorder, caused by the indifference of [self-]interested managers; there are administrations with large funds at their disposal, where each official neglects all save his interests and ambition; there are libraries where all is disordered or destroyed, where we cannot understand either the employment of the income or the disposition of the books; there are streets which we cannot pass without terror or abhorrence from uncleanliness poisoning the air, and from the houses of drunkenness and disorder which encumber them; there are courts of justice, dedicated to the greatest of all the functions of government, through the incapacity of officials ruled by a chaos of disorder and injustice; there are departments from which the officials are absent; churches, a lamp unto the people forsaken and closed, without service or song, or from which, through the irregularity of their services, the worshippers bring away nothing save confusion, ignorance, and irritation ... There lies the real need of our time, which we sacrifice to abstract questions and sounding words ...

K.P. Pobedonostsev, [10], pp. 117–21.

DOCUMENT 3   **VILLAGE DRINKING**

Pioneer ethnographer Olga Semyonova spent four years observing life in Russian villages at the turn of the century. Here she describes the important social role played by vodka consumption.

[Among the peasantry] Drinking is a temptation no one can withstand. Prodigious amounts of alcohol are consumed at wedding parties. I myself have attended weddings at which nine- and ten-year-old girls were made to drink so that they would dance for everyone's entertainment. Reportedly they make the boys drink 'for fun', too. Most youngsters start drinking on a dare.

There are some occasions at which drunkenness is required by tradition. For example, young men are expected to drink before they are drafted ... The revelry takes place both in the tavern and in the streets, and is accompanied by much rowdiness. All the [future conscripts] are supposed to carry accordions, which they play all night long, right up to sunrise. With this accompaniment to their drunken singing, the whole crowd stalks around the village, smashing window panes and indulging in most unseemly pranks. These capers are regarded with tolerance ...

The best occasion for young people to get drunk for the first time is the annual festival, which in this region takes place in connection with St. Michael's Day. On that holiday, every person in the parish is drunk. In a good year the festival lasts for a week, but even when the crops are poor, people manage to go on a spree for three days. There is also a great deal of drinking at Shrovetide. This is the time for traveling to visit relatives, and for riding troikas. Accidents abound in the springtime [as a result of drunkenness]. Some people drown in water-filled ravines. Others are crushed under falling wagons; a drunken peasant will have a wagon tip over on him, and that is the end of him. Considerably less drinking occurs on Christmas and Easter …

A young man may be introduced to heavy drinking during the street parties. Street parties provide a brisk trade for the bootleg establishment that is invariably operated in every village, usually by some widow. The drinks are served in a shkalik, a mediumsized glass containing approximately two ounces. A moderate drinker will order two or three shkaliks in a row. Peasants claim they drink 'to drown their sorrows' or 'to ease their troubled minds.' Frequently vodka becomes indispensable for them. At meetings of the village council, it is customary to take turns paying for drinks. When visiting someone's house, a peasant will be pleased with the refreshments only if a fair amount of alcohol is served. Snacks are of much less concern. Peasants are naturally more willing to drink while on a visit or in a tavern than at home. When there is a bootleg establishment in the village, men are not likely to drink at all at home, except at family occasions, such as weddings and baptismal dinners.

Drinking also accompanies delivery of the first load of grain for grinding. The miller provides the liquor, for which he is repaid with grain. Another occasion for general drunkenness is seasonal field work for the landlord (usually mowing and transportation of produce to town), who by way of payment treats the peasants to refreshments. On these occasions dreadful fights break out and can result in maiming or even killing with a scythe. When the oats are taken to town for sale, the occasion is celebrated with drinking. Needless to say, service in the army is also a school for drinking. When a group of young horseherds includes a few older boys, say about age sixteen or seventeen, they instruct the younger ones to steal liquor from home when their parents are away. The loot is then shared by all, not infrequently including boys ten to twelve years old.

O. Semyonova Tian-Shanskaia, [12], pp. 110–12.

DOCUMENT 4   THE KHODYNKA DISASTER

A young apprentice, Semën Kanatchikov, left this eyewitness account of the disaster and its repercussions.

Either on the 14th or 15th of May, a big public celebration was announced, to be held on the Khodynka field. It was said that during the festivities little bundles filled with sausages, rolls, a mug bearing the emblem of the tsar, and a half-ruble piece would be distributed to everyone from special booths. No one could say with any accuracy just what kind of mug it would be: some said copper, others said tin or porcelain.

On the day before the celebration, Krasnitsky, the master mechanic at our factory, gathered together the foremen of all the shops to announce that, in order to avoid the big crush, all our workers were to start off for Khodynka at eight in the morning in a single group led by him ... We began to grow agitated and to speak rudely about the master mechanic, fearing that by the time we got to the field all the gifts would already be distributed. Some of the men proposed to leave immediately and spend the night there. Vanka and I were fully prepared to go in the evening, but Korovin, who had complete faith in Krasnitsky's promises, would not allow it.

It is a clear and sunny morning. Commanded by master mechanic Krasnitsky, we march in a long file to the Khodynka field. The morning air is bracing, the sun shines brightly, there is laughter, joking, animated talk, and, at the end of our path, crowds of joyful people making merry, puppet shows, music, folkdancing, singing, the brash, endless sounds of the accordion, and so on. And then, suddenly ...

As we approach the vicinity of Khodynka, we encounter a cabman. In his cab a young woman is tossing about and screaming something incomprehensible at the top of her lungs. 'Nervous hysteria, most likely,' we decide, and we continue our procession ...

Then some people approached our group, shouting: 'Oh my God, oh my God! How many people have been crushed! They're taking away the corpses by cartloads!'

'Who!? How were they crushed?'

'You can't imagine how many people fell into the wells! There's this deep, deep well; people kept falling into it even when it was already packed,' others told us. 'They say the wells were left open on purpose!'

'There was this enormous crowd there, swaying from side to side, moving like waves in the sea,' says another, 'and you could see the steam from the stuffy air hovering over the crowd. And all the people standing there, just as if everyone was still alive, but when the crowd finally gives way, suddenly they fall to the ground by the hundreds: their crushed bodies had been standing up.'

'The only reason I'm still alive is because I managed to make my way through by practically climbing over everyone's head. A kind person came by and put me down on a safe, high spot,' said a small, skinny man in a visored cap.

We never received our gifts and we were certainly in no mood for them anyway. We were happy and thankful that we hadn't left for the field in the evening and hadn't ended up in that mess ourselves. On the way back home, now and then we would run into military wagons piled with corpses covered with bast mats; arms, legs, and heads could be seen dangling out from under the mats ... It was terrifying.

On the following day the crush at Khodynka was the only thing discussed at our factory. The newspapers were beginning to publish lists of the victims. Some of the workers found the names of their friends. A low murmur began to arise. The atmosphere grew tense. The lists that appeared in the papers clearly underestimated the number of victims, placing it at two or three hundred, I can't remember exactly. This evoked enormous outrage.

'The papers are lying. They crushed thirty thousand, not three hundred, the dogs!' the old worker Smirnov, whose friend or relative had been killed, said angrily. 'Have you ever heard of anything like it? Thousands of people are crushed to death and they don't even find the guilty party!' ...

Although it had no direct relation to the shop-floor interests of the workers of our factory, the Khodynka catastrophe greatly weakened the authority of our rulers and undermined the old blind faith in the tsar, even among the older men. What aroused people's indignation most of all was the irresponsibility, the impunity of the authorities who had destroyed thousands of lives.

R.E. Zelnik (ed. and trans.), [15], pp. 41–5.

DOCUMENT 5   WITTE AND THE ZEMSTVOS

According to V.I. Gurko, a senior official in the Ministry of the Interior, the basis of Witte's hostility towards zemstvo institutions was his desire to see Russia transformed by industrial capitalism.

Witte was but a son of his time; a fervent admirer of the capitalistic structure of society and of capitalism in general. But in his mind this capitalism was connected with industry and not with agriculture ... Witte's hostile attitude toward the agricultural elements and the representatives of the landed gentry was carried over from them to the zemstvo, which rested exclusively on these elements. In 1899 he made a report concerning the project to establish zemstvo institutions in the western gubernias, and in this report he tried to establish the idea that under an autocracy the zemstvo was an ineffective and dangerous administrative organization, and pronounced himself definitely for the curtailment of its activities ... Of the cultural role of the zemstvos, the importance of which no one has ever denied, Witte said not a word; on the contrary he insisted that the zemstvos were 'overtaxing the peasantry.'

But Witte's animosity to the zemstvos was caused by something more than his hostility to the landed gentry. The zemstvos enjoyed the privilege of levying their own taxes. As this did not accord with Witte's policy of directing the greatest possible amount of the public wealth into the state treasury, he endeavored to curtail this zemstvo privilege. It was to this end that he tried to deprive the zemstvos of their administration of public education ...

One of Witte's glaring inconsistencies can be seen in a comparison of his attitude to the zemstvos on the one hand and to the municipal administrations on the other. The latter as well as the former had the right to levy taxes; and actually both organizations were anomalous in an autocratic regime. But Witte never opposed the municipal administration because he never opposed the industrial classes. Not only did he refrain from handicapping any sort of social organization allied to industry but often he endeavored to increase its strength.

V.I. Gurko, [3], pp. 60–4.

DOCUMENT 6   **OFFICIALDOM AND ANTISEMITISM**

At a January, 1903 meeting of the Committee of Ministers, V.K. Plehve, Minister of the Interior, put his antisemitic views on record.

I consider Jewry a phenomenon hostile to the national and state well-being of Russia. The characteristics of the Jews and the manifestations of their activities, which are hostilely directed against the government and the existing order, are of such seriousness that the government not only has the right but even the obligation to impose binding irksome measures on them and not give them an equal position with the Christian population. From this point of view I am in complete solidarity with the views of my predecessor, and I consider any weakening of the measures taken against Jewry as not in conformity with the views and tasks of the government.

J. Schneiderman, [98], p. 279.

DOCUMENT 7   **BOBRIKOV'S PLANS FOR FINLAND**

An extract from Bobrikov's diary, published in Helsinki after his death at the hands of an assassin.

Finland, having been conquered by Russian arms, has come into Russian possession in accordance with the rights of conquest ... as from 1809 the country has belonged to the Russian Empire and ... is forever united with it. Its inhabitants are irrefutably Russian citizens and subjects of the Tsar of All the Russias.

The conquest of Finland was necessitated by the need to move our northern frontier further away from Petersburg. But despite an association of ninety years, the purpose of this conquest has to date not been achieved ... In the place of a foreign state a frontier area has been created which has up to now remained alien to its benefactor, Russia, and openly seeks to establish its rights as a constitutional state, united to Russia simply by a common supreme authority.

The Finnish frontier country is today as foreign to us as it was during the time before its conquest.

Under such circumstances it is not easy for the representative of Russian authority in Finland, in addition to looking after the interests of the state, to find common ground with the present experts of the country in this field and to get to work on these matters. It will take not a little time to study the question on the spot and then to clarify and establish the system which best meets the main interests of the state.

In order to achieve the most thorough and comprehensive investigation of Finland's present position, it is essential that a revision [investigating committee] similar to that carried out [in 1882–4] by Senator Manassein in the Baltic provinces be performed by Russians. Finnish separatism could however be limited before the results of this revision are published by (1) carrying out an amalgamation of the army together with an adjustment of the burden and costs of maintenance of troops; a reformation of the Finnish Cadet Corps in a Russian manner; the establishment in Helsinki of an officers' club for Russian and Finnish officers (2) abolishing or limiting the importance of the State-Secretariat, in addition to which the Governor-General shall be accorded the right, albeit in matters of particular importance, to be present at the submission of reports by the Minister State-Secretary (3) carrying out a codification of the laws of the land and establishing a special procedure for the inspection of matters which are common to the Empire and Grand Duchy (4) introducing the Russian language into the Senate, schools and civil service (5) permitting Russians to enter into service in the institutions of the Grand Duchy without the [language] qualifications imposed on them in this respect by the law of 1858 (6) arranging for supervision of the university and inspection of all textbooks used in Finnish schools (7) abolition of the separate customs and coinage institutions (8) founding an official Russian newspaper and permitting Russians to publish newspapers in Russian or one of the local languages (9) simplifying the present ceremonial followed at the opening of the Diet (10) modifying the instructions provided in 1812 for the Governor-General ...

D.G. Kirby, [5], pp. 77–8.

DOCUMENT 8   **THE FIRST ISSUE OF** *Liberation*

This declaration of editorial policy, written by Peter Struve, appeared in the first issue, on 18 June / 1 July 1902.

We shall preach not accomodation to the existing political regime, which saps the best energies of the nation, but, on the contrary, the struggle against it. We shall not skirt diplomatically all the conclusions which follow from the demand for political freedom ... Our task is not to divide but to unite. The cultural and political liberation of Russia can be neither the monopoly nor the main burden of a single class, a single party, a single doctrine. It must become a national cause embracing all the people, one that will evoke a response from every heart capable of distinguishing between what is moral and what is amoral in politics, a heart which, for that reason, is unwilling to come to terms with the violence and arbitrariness of a band of bureaucrats who administer a great people without being subjected to any controls and without owing any responsibility.

R. Pipes, [81], p. 319.

DOCUMENT 9   **THE UNION OF LIBERATION**

This resolution was adopted at its founding congress in January, 1904.

The Union of Liberation assumes as its first and principal task the political liberation of Russia. The Union regards political freedom even in its most minimal dimensions as utterly incompatible with the absolutist character of the Russian monarchy, and for that reason it will struggle above all for the liquidation of autocracy and the establishment in Russia of a constitutional regime. In defending the concrete forms which the constitutional regime can assume in Russia, the Union of Liberation will exert all its efforts to see to it that the political problem is solved in the spirit of broad democracy. It recognizes above all that in essence it is indispensable to place at the foundation of political reform the principle of a universal, equal, secret, and direct vote.

While placing prime emphasis on political demands, the Union of Liberation acknowledges the necessity of defining the principles underlying its attitude toward the socioeconomic problems which life itself brings to the fore. In the realm of socioeconomic policy, the Union will be guided by the same basic principle of democratism, assigning its activity the direct aim of defending the interests of the working class.

As pertains to the national question, the Union recognizes the right to self-determination of the various nationalities living in the Russian state. In regard to Finland, the Union identifies itself with the demand for the restitution of the constitutional order prevailing there until illegally violated during the present reign.

R. Pipes, [81], pp. 335–6.

DOCUMENT 10   A ROYAL FLEA-BITE

Prince Urusov, the newly-appointed governor of troubled Bessarabia, was astonished by the tsar's complacent reaction to the Japanese attack on Port Arthur.

Prior to my departure ... I presented myself to the Emperor at the Winter Palace. Before the audience I met Mr. Krupenskii, the Marshal of Nobility of Bessarabia province, whose audience with the Emperor preceded my own. He told me that the emotion he had shown regarding the gravity of these events, his fear of their consequences, his irritation at the backhanded way in which the enemy had declared war – all had been met with calm and indifference by [the Emperor] who assured him that at court the Japanese attack was considered no more than a 'flea-bite'.

The Emperor's tranquil, almost cheerful manner struck me as soon as I entered his office ... [When] I spoke of the misfortune which was befalling Russia as a result of this unexpected war ... [he replied] 'I am entirely at ease about the outcome of this war ... as for you, your task will become easier from now on.' Since I could not immediately grasp his train of thought, he explained to me that because the war was producing an explosion of patriotism, anti-government agitation would by the same token be reduced, and that consequently, if troubles were to break out anywhere, the authorities would easily re-establish order.

S.D. Ouroussof (Urusov), [9], pp. 273–4.

DOCUMENT 11   FATHER GAPON'S PETITION

Note the distinctly radical tone of the passages in italics, which were added to the final version of the text only two days before the 9 January, 1905 demonstration.

A Most Humble and Loyal Address
of the Workers of St. Petersburg Intended for Presentation
to HIS MAJESTY on Sunday at two o'clock on the Winter Palace Square

SIRE:

We, the workers *and inhabitants of* St. Petersburg, *of various estates*, our wives, our children, and our aged, helpless parents, come to Thee, O SIRE, to seek justice and protection. We are impoverished; we are oppressed, overburdened with excessive toil, contemptuously treated. We are not even recognized as human beings, but are treated like slaves who must suffer their bitter fate in silence and without complaint. And we have suffered, but even so we are being further ... pushed into the slough of poverty, arbitrariness, and ignorance. We are suffocating in despotism and lawlessness. O SIRE, we have no strength left, and our endurance is at an end. We have reached that frightful moment when death is better than the prolongation of our unbearable sufferings.

Hence, we stopped work and told our employers that we will not resume work until our demands are fulfilled. We did not ask much; we sought only that without which there is no life for us but hard labor and eternal suffering. Our first request was that our employers agree to discuss our needs with us. But ... this we were refused. We were prohibited even from speaking of our needs, since no such right is given us by law. The following requests were also deemed to be outside of the law: the reduction of the workday to eight hours; our mutual participation in determining the rates for our work and in the settlement of grievances that might arise between us and the lower managerial staff; to raise the minimum daily wages for unskilled workers, and for women as well, to one ruble; to abolish overtime work; to give our sick better medical attention without insults; and to arrange our workshops so that we might work there without encountering death from murderous drafts, rain, and snow.

According to our employers and managers, our demands turned out to be illegal, our every request a crime, and our desire to improve our conditions an insolence, insulting to them ... O SIRE ... *we are many thousands* here, but we are human beings in appearance only, for we, *with the rest of the Russian people*, do not possess a single human right, not even the right to speak, think, gather, discuss our needs and take steps to improve our conditions. *We are enslaved, enslaved under the patronage and with the aid of Thy officials.* Anyone of us who dares to raise his voice in defense of the working class and *the people* is thrown into jail or exiled. Kindheartedness is punished as a crime. To feel sorry for a ... downtrodden, maltreated human being bereft of his rights is to commit a heinous crime! *The workers and the peasants are delivered into the hands of the bureaucratic administration, comprised of embezzlers of public funds and robbers, who not only care nothing for the needs of the people, but flagrantly abuse them. The bureaucratic administration brought the country to the brink of ruin, involved her in a humiliating war, and is leading Russia closer and closer to disaster. We, the workers and people, have no voice whatsoever in the spending of huge sums collected from us in taxes. We do not even know how the money, collected from the impoverished people, is spent. The people are deprived of the opportunity to express their wishes and demands, to participate in the establishment of taxes and public spending. The workers are deprived of the opportunity to organize into unions in order to defend their interests.*

O SIRE, is this in accordance with God's laws, by the grace of which Thou reignest? Is it possible to live under such laws? Would it not be preferable for all of us, the toiling people of Russia, to die? Let the capitalists-*exploiters of the working class* and officials, the embezzlers and plunderers of the Russian people, live and enjoy their lives.

These are the prospects that are before us, SIRE, and the reasons that brought us to the walls of Thy palace. Here we seek the final salvation. Do not turn Thy help away from Thy people. Lead them out from the mire of lawlessness, poverty, and ignorance. Allow them to determine their own future; deliver them from the intolerable oppression of the officialdom. Raze the wall that separates Thee from Thy people and rule the country with them. Thou reignest in order to bring happiness to Thy people, but this happiness is torn out of our hands by Thy officials, and there is nothing left for us but grief and humiliation ... Consider our demands attentively and without anger, for they are uttered not in malice but for the good, ours as well as Thine, O SIRE. We speak not in insolence, but from the realization of the necessity to find a way out of a situation intolerable to us all. Russia is too vast, and her needs are too great and manifold to be dealt with exclusively by the bureaucrats. *Popular representation is essential;* it is essential that the people help themselves and *govern themselves.* Truly, only they know their *real* needs. Refuse not their help, accept it ... and command representatives of the Russian land, of all her classes, of all her [legal] estates, *as well as representatives of the workers*, to gather without delay. Let these include a capitalist, worker, official, priest, doctor, teacher – let everyone, whoever he may be, elect his representative. Let everyone be free and equal in his choice, and for this purpose let the elections to the constituent assembly be conducted under conditions of universal ... secret, and equal suffrage.

This is our principal request, upon which everything else depends. This is the main and the only balm for our ...wounds, without which they will continue to fester and will *soon* bring us death.

But a single measure cannot heal ... our wounds. Others are needed, and we have come to Thee, SIRE openly and directly as to the father, to tell Thee, *in the name of the entire toiling class of Russia*, that the following are essential:

I. Measures to eliminate the ignorance of and arbitrariness toward the Russian people.

1. The immediate release and return of those who suffered for their political and religious convictions, for strikes and peasant disorders.
2. An *immediate* proclamation of freedom and inviolability of the person, freedom of speech, press, association, and worship.
3. Free universal and compulsory public education, financed by the State.
4. Responsibility of the ministers before the people and guarantees that the government will act according to law.
5. Equality of all before the law without any exceptions.
6. *Separation of the church from the state.*

II. Measures to eliminate the poverty of the people.

1. Abolition of indirect taxation and the introduction of a progressive income tax.
2. Abolition of the land redemption payments, cheap credit, and the gradual transfer of the land to the people.

3. *Contracts for orders of the war and naval departments are to be made in Russia and not abroad.*
4. *Termination of the war in accordance with the will of the people.*

III. Measures to eliminate the oppression of labor by capital.

1. *Abolition of the system of factory inspectors.*
2. *Establishment in factories and plants of permanent elected worker committees, which are to participate with management in the consideration of worker grievances. Workers must not be discharged without the consent of these committees.*
3. Freedom of co-operative associations and professional worker unions *is to be allowed without delay.*
4. An eight-hour workday and strict regulation of overtime work.
5. Freedom of the struggle for labor against capital *is to be allowed without delay.*
6. *Immediate* establishment of normal wage rates.
7. Participation of representatives of the ..*working classes* in the drafting of a bill for state insurance of workers is *indispensable, and is to be put into effect without delay.*

Here, O SIRE, are our principal needs which we have come to lay before Thee ... *only with their fulfillment can our Motherland be emancipated from slavery and poverty, only then can she prosper, and only then can the workers unite in order to defend their interests against the brazen exploitation of the capitalists and the plundering, stifling bureaucratic administration.*
Issue Thy orders and swear to fulfill them, and Thou wilt make Russia happy and glorious, and Thy name will forever be engraved in our hearts and in the hearts of all our descendants. But if Thou withholdest Thy command and failest to respond to our supplications, we will die here on this square before Thy palace. There is no place for us to go, nor is there any reason for us to go any further ... There are two paths before us: one to freedom and happiness, the other into the grave. ... Let our lives be a sacrifice for suffering Russia. We do not regret this sacrifice, but offer it gladly.

W. Sablinsky, [97], pp. 344–9.

DOCUMENT 12   STRUVE'S REACTION TO THE OCTOBER MANIFESTO

A colleague who worked on the editorial staff of Liberation *in Paris recalls Struve's single-minded preoccupation with events in Russia.*

He ran ten times a day to the newspaper kiosk at the metro station, grabbing all editions: morning, evening, early, late, noontime, and afternoon, regular and extra. These were put out by all the newspapers. Whole pages were full of Russia, and each brought new details confirming the vehemence of the movement. Struve walked the streets ... the paper open in front of him like a shield, risking falls under carriages, bumping into passers-by, impervious to their deserved abuse. At home, he looked senselessly into all the rooms, muttered incomprehensible words, stared at us with unseeing eyes ...

Suddenly, on the evening of October 17, extra editions came out bearing in enormous letters the memorable words: 'The Tsar Gives In – Concedes Constitution.'

Just that day [Struve's wife] Nina was in labor with her fifth child. She did not go to a hospital but stayed home to carry on her usual work. As befitted the wife of the editor of a constitutional journal, she chose for her delivery the memorable day of October 17, the day of the constitution ...

A disheveled Struve, shaking a pile of newspapers, shoving everyone aside, burst into the bedroom where his wife was straining in the last pangs of childbirth.

'Nina! Constitution!'

The midwife took him by the arm and pushed him out of the bedroom. Half an hour later, the fifth Struve was born.

R. Pipes, [81], pp. 388–9.

DOCUMENT 13   DISSOLUTION OF THE FIRST DUMA

According to V.A. Maklakov, a right-wing member of the Constitutional-Democratic (Kadet) Party, his colleagues were stunned when the government's decision to dissolve the First Duma failed to produce a nationwide uprising.

The untimely dissolution of parliament is always an exceptional event, but it is foreseen by all constitutions and is not considered catastrophic. However, as Stolypin warned, the dissolution of the First Duma was regarded as a state upheaval and was a shock indeed. Everyone believed that the country must reply immediately, as though it had met some challenge. The First Duma self-confidently predicted all along that the country awaited only a signal to depose the powerless government, and if any encroachment should be made on the Duma, nothing would be left of the government. 'The dissolution of the Duma,' wrote Miliukov confidently on July 6, 'is the equivalent of civil war.' Then dissolution came, and to everyone's amazement, the country remained calm.

Sensitive people could not grasp this passive acceptance. The wise and matter-of-fact [Kadet deputy Maksim] Vinaver, whose admiration of the Duma diminished his customary far-sightedness, could not believe his eyes after the dissolution. He tells about that morning as follows: 'on my way to visit [his colleague] Petrunkevich I looked about me; searched in other people's faces and in inanimate stones for the reflection of our disaster. Sleepy pedestrians, sleepy horses, a sleepy sun; desolation; no life, no signs of movement. I wanted to scream in anguish and horror.'

Though I was in the country at the time ... I remember distinctly the impression of that day. A telegram delivered in the morning stated, 'The Duma dissolved. Stolypin premier.' That there was nothing resembling agitation among the peasants was quite understandable. But toward evening – it was a holiday – many visitors came from Moscow. All who came from the center were amazed at the imperturbable calm of the city, for we had not forgotten the stormy reaction to lesser events: the general strike and the barricades. We expected at least a railway stoppage, agitation, and excitement in the streets, but everything was calm. This seemed so improbable that we continued to hope; we waited not for the superficial simmer in the thin layer of the intelligentsia but for the profound, elemental upheaval...

[When on July 19 the Sveaborg garrison rebelled it seemed that ...] The country was awakening at last. But the illusion did not last long. The people remained indifferent, and neither heroic military revolts nor the terrible terrorist act [an explosion at Stolypin's villa] on Aptekar Island moved them. I was told by military people who put down the uprising how unexpectedly easy it was to crush it. After the preliminary success the rebels understood that they were alone and defended themselves without enthusiasm. No revolutionary dynamic was found in the country, or else it was so weak that Stolypin's police measures proved stronger. Yet the tactics of the First Duma were determined by its reliance on an invincible revolutionary uprising, which was even considered the duty of the country.

V.A. Maklakov, [6], pp. 219–21.

DOCUMENT 14   THE CRISIS OF THE OLD INTELLIGENTSIA

In his contribution to the Vekhi symposium published in 1909, former Marxist Semën Frank offered a stinging critique of the moral outlook of the Russian intelligentsia.

The total sterility and impotence of the intelligentsia's consciousness when it came into contact with the real forces of life, and, on the other hand, the moral rottenness which practical activity revealed in some of its roots, are symptoms that cannot disappear without a trace. Indeed, we are witnessing the collapse and disintegration of the traditional intelligentsia spirit. The Russian *intelligent* as ... a complete and integral moral character-type despite all his contradictions, is beginning to disappear before our eyes and soon will exist only as an ideal ... [Indeed] only rarely is it embodied in pure form in the younger generation. Right now everything is confused: the Social democrats are discussing God, studying aesthetics, fraternizing with 'mystical anarchists', losing faith in materialism, and reconciling Marx with Mach and

Nietzsche; a peculiar mystical socialism is becoming popular in the guise of syndicalism; 'class interests' are somehow being combined with the 'sex problem' and decadent poetry. Only a few old representatives of the classical Populism of the seventies wander about despondently and futilely in this dissonant babel of tongues and beliefs, like the last members of a once-powerful but now unproductive and soon-to-be-extinct cultural species.

There is no reason to be surprised at this crisis of the old intelligentsia consciousness, and still less to be grieved. On the contrary, we should be surprised at how slowly and unconsciously it is proceeding, more like an involuntary organic disease than a conscious cultural and philosophical reorganization. And there is cause for regret that despite the steady disintegration of the old faith, new ideas and ideals are emerging too weakly and vaguely, so that we cannot yet foresee the end of the crisis ...

Perhaps the most remarkable trait of the recent Russian social movement, and one that has had a telling impact on its fate, is its *lack of philosophical reflection and understanding*. Such historical movements as, for example, the great English or French revolutions tried to bring to life new, independently reasoned and developed philosophical ideas and values, and to lead national life onto the still untrodden paths revealed by the profound, bold investigations of creative political thought. Our social movement, by contrast, was guided by old themes which had been taken on faith, and not even from their original sources but at second- or third-hand. The absence of independent intellectual activity in our social movement, its profound philosophical conservatism, is so generally acknowledged and undisputed that it attracts scarcely any attention and is considered natural and normal.

The socialist idea that dominates our intelligentsia's mind was adopted whole, without criticism or reflection, in the form in which it had crystallized in the West after a century of intellectual ferment. Its roots go back to the individualistic rationalism of the eighteenth century, on the one hand, and, on the other, to the philosophy of reactionary romanticism that arose out of intellectual dismay at the outcome of the great French Revolution. In believing in Lassalle and Marx, essentially we are believing in the values and ideas developed by Rousseau and de Maistre, Holbach and Hegel, Burke and Bentham; we are feeding on scraps from the philosophical table of the eighteenth and early nineteenth centuries. And when we assimilate these venerable ideas, the majority of which are already more than a century old, we pay absolutely no attention to these roots; we use the fruits without even asking from what tree they were picked, and we blindly assert their value without questioning their foundations. It is very typical of this philosophical mindlessness that of all the formulations of socialism the one that acquired overwhelming sovereignty over our minds was Marx's doctrine – a system which, despite the breadth of its scientific structure, not only lacks any philosophical and ethical basis whatsoever, but rejects it on principle.

M.S. Shatz and J.E. Zimmerman (eds), [13], pp. 153–4.

DOCUMENT 15   **GUCHKOV WARNS OF AN IMPENDING CATASTROPHE**

Alexander Guchkov, leader of the moderate Octobrists, sounded the alarm at a party conference held in November, 1913.

What is to be the issue of the grave crisis through which we are now passing? What does the encroachment of reaction bring with it? Whither is the government policy, or rather lack of policy, carrying us?

Towards an inevitable and grave catastrophe! In this general forecast all are agreed; people of the most sharply opposed political views, of the most varied social groups, all agree with a rare, an unprecedented unanimity. Even representatives of the government, of that government which is the chief offender against the Russian people, are prepared to agree to this forecast, and their official and obligatory optimism ill conceals their inward alarm.

When will the catastrophe take effect? What forms will it assume? Who can foretell? Some scan the horizon with joyful anticipation, others with dread. But greatly do those err who calculate that on the ruins of the demolished system will arise that order which corresponds to their particular political and social views. In those forces that seem likely to come to the top in the approaching struggle, I do not see stable elements that would guarantee any kind of permanent political order. Are we not rather in danger of being plunged into a period of protracted, chronic anarchy which will lead to the dissolution of the Empire? Shall we not again pass through a Time of Troubles, only under new and more dangerous international conditions? ...

Once in the days of the people's madness we [Octobrists] raised our sobering voice against the excesses of radicalism. In the[se] days of the madness of the government it is we who should speak to the government a grave word of warning. We once believed and invited others to believe; we patiently waited. Now we must declare that our patience is exhausted, and with our patience our faith; at such a moment as this we must not leave to the professional Opposition, to the radical and socialist parties, the monopoly of opposing the government and the ruinous policy it has adopted; for in doing so we should create the dangerous illusion that the government is combating radical utopias and social experiments – whereas it is opposing the satisfaction of the most moderate and elementary demands of public opinion, demands that were at one time admitted by the government itself. Before the approaching catastrophe it is we who should make the final attempt to bring the government to reason, to open its eyes, to awaken in it the alarm that we so strongly feel. For we are the representatives of those propertied classes, all the vital interests of which are bound up with the peaceful evolution of the State, and on which in the case of disaster the first blow will fall ...

The danger of the present moment lies, in fact, not in the revolutionary parties, not in anti-monarchical propaganda, not in anti-religious teaching, not in the dissemination of the ideas of socialism and anti-militarism, not in the agitation of anarchists against the government. The historical drama through which we are now passing lies in the fact that we are compelled to uphold the monarchy against those who are the natural defenders of the monarchical principle, we are compelled to uphold the Church against the ecclesiastical hierarchy, the army against its leaders, the authority of the government against the government itself. We seemed to have sunk into a state of public despondency and apathy, a passive condition. But thence it is only one step to despair, which is an active force of tremendously destructive quality. May God avert from our country the danger that overshadows it.

A.I. Guchkov, [4], pp. 151–2, 156–8.

DOCUMENT 16   PATRIOTIC ENTHUSIASM

The bombastic President of the Fourth Duma, M. V. Rodzianko, describes the official St Petersburg's response to the tsar's delaration of war.

On the day that the Emperor issued the manifesto announcing a state of war with Germany, huge crowds assembled in front of the Winter Palace. After a special service in the chapel, the Emperor spoke a few words to the assembly in the Palace, concluding with the solemn promise not to lay down arms while a single span of Russian land remained in the enemy's hand. Thundering cheers resounded through the Palace and were taken up by the crowds outside. The Emperor came out on to the balcony, followed by the Empress. A vast crowd filled the whole square and all the adjacent streets. At the sight of the Emperor, an electric current seemed to pass through the mass of people; a mighty 'hurrah' filled the air. Banners and placards, on which were inscribed the words 'Long live Russia and the Slavonic cause,' were lowered to the ground, and the whole crowd, as one man, fell on their knees before the Emperor. He tried to speak, raised his hand: the front rows endeavoured to silence the rest, but nothing could be heard amid the deafening cheers and roaring of the crowd. The Emperor stood for a while with bowed head, overpowered by the solemnity of the moment, when Tsar and people became one. Then he turned slowly, and withdrew into his apartments.

On leaving the Palace we mingled with the crowd of demonstrators, and came across some factory workers. I stopped them and asked how they came to be here, when they had been on strike, and almost on the point of an armed rising a short time ago. The workmen replied: 'That was our own family dispute. We thought reforms came too slowly through the Duma. But now all Russia is involved. We have rallied to our Tsar as to our emblem, and we shall follow him for the sake of victory over the Germans.'

The Imperial Duma and the [State] Council of the Empire were convened on July 26 (Old style), 1914. Before the session the members of both Chambers were received at the Winter Palace by the Emperor ... Everyone was stirred to patriotic enthusiasm, and party differences were forgotten. All the

Ministers of the Crown, the highest dignitaries of the Court, the whole Council of the Empire, and the Imperial Duma were assembled in the great Nicolaevsky Hall. The Emperor entered accompanied by the Commander-in-Chief, the Grand Duke Nicolai Nicolaevitch, and addressed the assembly in the following words:

'I welcome you in these solemn and anxious days through which all Russia is passing. Germany, followed by Austria, has declared war on Russia. The great wave of patriotism and loyalty to the Throne which has swept our native land is to me, and presumably also to you, a token that our great Mother Russia will carry on that war, sent as a visitation by God, to its desired consummation. This unanimous impulse of love on the part of my people and their readiness to sacrifice everything, even life itself, give me the necessary strength, calmly and steadfastly to anticipate the future. We are not merely defending our honour and dignity within the confines of our own country, but are fighting for our congenital brother-Slavs. I rejoice to see that at this solemn moment the Slavs are being so closely and indissolubly united with Russia. I am certain that each of you, at your respective posts, will help me to bear the trials which are sent us, and that we all, beginning with myself, will do our duty to the end. Great is the God of the Russian land.'

Ringing cheers resounded through the hall ... [I replied]

'Your Imperial Majesty: It was with a feeling of profound emotion and pride that Russia heard the call of the Russian Tsar summoning his people to be one with him in the solemn hour of trial sent to our Motherland... .

The representatives of the people, called into political being by the will of your Majesty, now stand before you. The Imperial Duma, which embodies in itself the unanimous impulse of all Russia's component parts and united in a singleness of purpose, has empowered me to tell you, Sire, that your people are ready to take up arms for the honour and glory of the Motherland. Without differences of opinion, views and convictions, the Imperial Duma, speaking in the name of the whole Russian nation, says calmly and firmly to her Tsar: "Sire, be of good cheer, the Russian people are with you. With a firm belief in the grace of God, they will grudge no sacrifice until the foe is vanquished and Russia's honour vindicated."'

The Emperor's eyes were full of tears. He replied:

'I thank you from my heart, I thank you, gentlemen, for your patriotic spirit, which I never doubted, and of which you have now given me actual proof. With all my heart I wish you every success. God is with us.'

The Emperor made the sign of the Cross; so did we all, and sang: "Lord, save thy people." The general enthusiasm was unbounded.

M.V. Rodzianko, [11], pp. 108–11.

DOCUMENT 17   **WAR ON THE ENEMY WITHIN**

Both the persistence of offically sponsored antisemitism and the wartime paralysis of civil government are captured in this note by A.N. Iakhontov, Secretary of the Council of Ministers.

From the moment that our retreat had started, the Council of Ministers constantly encountered the problem of the Jews. Headquarters became convinced that the Jewish population in the theater of war was a focus of espionage and help to the enemy. On this basis, it developed the idea of the necessity for clearing the frontal zone of all Jews. The application of this measure began in Galicia. The authorities in the rear began to send out, into the inner Russian provinces, thousands and tens of thousands of Austrian Jews. All this took place, of course, not voluntarily, but by force. The Jews were driven out *en masse*, without regard for sex or age. The common mass included the sick, the infirm, and even pregnant women. News of this action, and of the coercion which accompanied it, immediately spread throughout Russia and abroad. Influential Jewry raised the alarm. The Allied governments began to protest such a policy, and to point out its dangerous consequences. The Ministry of Finance began to encounter various difficulties in the conduct of financial operations. The Council of Ministers, in written form and also in oral communication of its chairman and of particular ministers, frequently called the attention of the Supreme Commander and General Ianushkevich to the necessity of stopping the persecution of the whole Jewish mass and ceasing the blanket accusations of treason, explaining that this was required both by internal and international considerations.

Nevertheless, Headquarters remained deaf to all arguments and evidence ... first of all in [the Baltic province of] Courland, and then in other localities, the enforced Jewish migration was carried out on a mass scale by especially appointed military units. What went on is indescribable. Even the most irreconcilable anti-Semites came to see the members of the government with protests and complaints against the outrageous treatment of the Jews at the front. And ultimately it became impossible to survive in the provinces within the zone of settlement into which the involuntary refugees, driven by the military authorities, were moved – not only for the ruined newcomers, but for the native population as well. All kinds of crises occurred: in supplies, in housing, and so forth. Epidemics began. In various localities the atmosphere became more and more dangerous; the Jews were angry at everyone and everything, while the local inhabitants were angry at the uninvited guests who, moreover, were being denounced as traitors and were angered by conditions under which it became impossible to survive in one's own home.

The Jewish intelligentsia, and the circles of the Russian public which are united with them, are utterly outraged. The press, the factions in the Duma, various organizations, and prominent individual representatives of Russian Jewry demand that the government take decisive steps to stop the mass persecutions. In the Allied countries, and particularly in [neutral] America, one hears heated appeals for aid to the suffering Jews in Russia. There are protest meetings about the policy of racial persecution, and so forth. The consequences of this movement: growing difficulty in obtaining credits, both in internal and external markets. The repercussions were greatest in our financial dealings with the United States, who, by that time, were becoming more and more influential as the banker of warring Europe.

M. Cherniavsky, [2], pp. 56–7.

DOCUMENT 18   **PROGRAMME OF THE PROGRESSIVE BLOC, 1915**

In August 1915, dissatisfaction with the government's apparent inability to organize the country for war brought together in the so-called Progressive Bloc most of the political parties in the Fourth Duma.

The undersigned representatives of factions and groups in the State Duma and State Council, believing (1) that only a strong, firm, and active government can lead our country to victory and (2) that such a government must be one which enjoys the confidence of the people and is capable of organizing cooperation between all citizens, have come to the unanimous conclusion that such cooperation can only be achieved, and the government gain sufficient authority if the following [minimum] conditions are observed.

1. The formation of a unified government of individuals who have the confidence of the country and are in agreement with the legislative institutions about the need for the rapid implementation of a definite programme.
2. A radical change in the present methods of administration, which are based on a distrust of initiative by the public, in particular:
   (a) strict observation of the principles of legality in government.
   (b) the removal of the dual authority of the military and the civil powers in questions which have no direct relevance to the execution of military operations.
   (c) the renewal of the system of local administration.
   (d) a rational and consistent policy to preserve internal peace, and the removal of discordances between nationalities and classes.

To implement this policy, the following administrative and legal measures must be taken.

1. The Imperial prerogative of mercy must be used to release those who are imprisoned for purely political or religious crimes, without having committed any other offences, and improvements must be made to the condition of others convicted of political or religious offences.

2. The release of those exiled by administrative order for political and religious offences.
3. A complete and definite halt to prosecutions undertaken, for whatever reason, on grounds of religion, and the withdrawal of circulars which have limited and altered the provisions of the edict of 17 April 1905.
4. The preparation of a bill to grant autonomy to Poland and its rapid introduction into the legislative institutions and, simultaneously, the removal of restrictions on the rights of Poles and a review of legislation on Polish landowning.
5. The process of repealing restrictive laws about Jews must be begun. Steps must be taken to abolish the Pale of settlement and the restrictions on Jewish entry to educational institutions and to various professions. The Jewish press should be revived.
6. A conciliatory policy towards Finland, in particular including changes in the make-up of the administration and the Senate, and the ending of legal action against officials.
7. The revival of the Ukrainian press, the release from imprisonment and exile of priests, convicted for belonging to the Uniate Church, and a revival of the question of exiled Galician inhabitants.
8. The revival of the activity of the trade unions and the ending of legal action against representatives of the workers' sickness funds on suspicion of their belonging to an illegal [political] party. The revival of the workers' press.
9. Agreement of the government and the legislative bodies on the rapid implementation of the following programme of bills, designed to organise the country to assist in victory and to maintain its internal peace: amendments to the zemstvo statute of 1890 and the municipal regulations of 1892, the introduction of a *volost* zemstvo, the introduction of zemstva in the borderlands ... A law on co-operatives. A bill on rest time for commercial employees. An improvement in the condition of post and telegraph workers. The permanent introduction of prohibition. A bill on zemstvo and municipal unions. A bill on changing from one religion to another. Regulations about inspections. The introduction of a local court in those provinces where this has been prevented for financial reasons. The implementation of legislative measures which are necessary to fulfil the above programme.

[Signed by representatives of the Kadets, Progressists, both Octobrist factions, the Centre group, and the progressive Nationalists.]

M. McCauley, [7], pp. 71–3.

GLOSSARY

gradonachalnik: the head of a city administration.

Holy Synod: the governing body of the Orthodox Church, 1721–1917, presided over by the Procurator-General.

land captains *(zemskie nachalniki):*   state officials, appointed by the Ministry of the Interior from among members of the local gentry, who from 1889 to 1917 exercised broad discretionary powers over peasant administration and justice.

narodniki: students, inspired by the ideology of revolutionary populism, who participated in the 'going to the people' movement in 1873–74.

nachalstvo: the authorities, 'the powers that be', 'the bosses'.

samodeiatelnost: any social activity that is spontaneously initiated and autonomously directed by those engaging in it.

soslovie: the traditional legal categorization of the tsar's subjects in one of four 'estates', nobility, clergy, townsmen, or peasants; rendered increasingly anachronistic by the pace of social change in the late nineteenth century.

Stavka: army field headquarters and the residence of the Commander-in-Chief, 1914–17.

village commune *(mir* or *obshchina):*   the basic institution of Russian village life, which exercised both administrative and economic responsibilities, e.g. periodic repartition of land, joint responsibility for taxes and other dues and levies.

volost: a small administrative-territorial division, comparable to a canton; after 1889 under the authority of a land captain.

zemskii sobor: 'Assembly of the Land', the proto-parliamentary body that flourished in Muscovite Russia from the mid-sixteenth to the mid-seventeenth centuries.

zemstvo: provincial and district self-governing institutions, 1864–1918, occupied largely with local economic administration; each comprised an executive board, an elected assembly, and salaried employees. In 1904–05 a vocal national zemstvo movement put itself at the forefront of Russian liberalism.

CHRONOLOGY OF EVENTS

1891–92   Famine and epidemics of cholera and typhus

1891   March, Construction of Trans-Siberian railway announced

1892   August, Witte appointed Minister of Finance

1894   January, Franco-Russian alliance
          November, Death of Alexander III, accession of Nicholas II

1895   May, Coronation of Nicholas II, Khodynka disaster
          October, St Petersburg Union of Struggle for the Emancipation
            of the Working Class formed

1896   Construction of Chinese Eastern railway

1902   Lenin's *What Is To Be Done?* published
          February, Anglo-Japanese Alliance
          Summer, Agrarian disturbances in southern Russia
          Socialist Revolutionary Party formed

1903   July/August, Brussels/London Congress of the Russian Social
            Democratic Workers' Party
          August, Witte discharged from Ministry of Finance

1904   January, Japanese naval attack on Port Arthur
            Union of Liberation formed
          June, Bobrikov, Governor-General of Finland, assassinated
          July, Plehve, Minister of the Interior, assassinated
          December, Fall of Port Arthur

1905   January, Bloody Sunday
          February, Battle of Mukden
            Nicholas II promises consultative assembly
          May, Battle of Tsushima

Founding Congress of the Union of Unions
Aug/Sept, Treaty of Portsmouth ends Russo-Japanese war
October, General strike begins in Moscow
Nicholas II's Manifesto promises elected State Duma and basic
civil liberties

1906   April/July, First Duma in session
July, Vyborg Manifesto

1907   February, Convocation of Second Duma
June, Dissolution of Second Duma
Stolypin's *coup*: Duma electoral law revised
November, Convocation of Third Duma (to June 1912)

1908   Bosnian crisis

1909   Publication of *Landmarks (Vekhi)*

1910   November, Funeral of Leo Tolstoi

1911   February, Kasso's purge of the universities
September, Stolypin assassinated

1912   April, Lena goldfields massacre
November, Convocation of Fourth Duma (to 1917)

1913   Beilis case

1914   July/Aug, Germany and Austria–Hungary declare war on Russia

1915   May, Formation of the War Industries Committees
August, Nicholas II becomes Commander-in-Chief
Programme of the Progressive Bloc published

1916   December, Rasputin murdered

1917   February, Demonstrations in Petrograd
Mutiny in the Petrograd Garrison
Provisional Committee of the Duma formed
Abdication of Nicholas II

GUIDE TO CHARACTERS

Alekseev, Admiral Evgenii Ivanovich (1843–1918): military commander and foreign policy maker; Viceroy of the Far East; commander of land and naval forces in the Russo-Japanese war until removed from command and from the vice-regency after the Mukden defeat.

Alexander III (Aleksandr Aleksandrovich) (1845–1894): Tsar/Emperor, reigned 1881–1894.

Alexandra (Aleksandra Feodorovna, b. Alix of Hesse-Darmstadt) (1872–1918): granddaughter of Queen Victoria, married Nicholas II, 1894; Tsarina/Empress, 1894–1917.

Beilis, Mendel (1874–1934): Jewish clerk employed in a brickworks in Kiev, accused in 1911 of murdering a Christian boy for ritual purposes; after two years in jail, tried and acquitted in October 1913. His trial aroused liberal opinion in Russia and attracted much foreign criticism of the tsarist regime.

Bezobrazov, Aleksandr Mikhailovich (1855–1931): a businessman with connections at Court who sought to use a timber concession in northern Korea as the basis for Russian expansion in the Far East; his actions aroused opposition in Japan and intensified the growing rivalry between Russia and Japan.

Bobrikov, Nikolai Ivanovich (1839–1904): as Governor-General of Finland, 1898–1904, he worked to destroy Finnish autonomy and to Russify the Grand Duchy; assassinated in June, 1904.

Bobrinskii, Count Aleksei Aleksandrovich (1852–1927): jurist; Marshal of Nobility of St Petersburg province; President of the Council of the United Nobility, 1906; elected to the Third Duma, 1907; subsequently a member of the Senate and the State Council.

Chernov, Viktor Mikhailovich (1873–1952): one of the founders of the Socialist Revolutionary (SR) party formed in 1902; as co-editor of its newspaper he endeavoured to synthesize Marxism and populism; helped to shape the party programme adopted in 1906.

Gapon, Georgii Appollonovich (1870–1906):   Orthodox priest and associate of Sergei Zubatov; organized the Assembly of Russian Factory and Mill Workers of St Petersburg in 1903; led the demonstration that resulted in the 'Bloody Sunday' massacre of 9 January, 1905; later became a double agent and was executed by revolutionaries in March, 1906.

Goremykin, Ivan Logginovich (1839–1917):   career bureaucrat; Assistant Minister of the Interior, 1895; Minister of the Interior, 1895–99; succeeded Witte as Chairman of the Council of Ministers, 1905–06; in obscurity until reappointed Chairman of the Council of Ministers, 1914–16.

Guchkov, Aleksandr Ivanovich (1862–1936):   public figure who in 1905 opposed Polish autonomy and supported the restoration of order; a founder of the moderate liberal Octobrist party; elected to Third Duma, 1907; headed Octobrist faction; President of Third Duma, 1910–11; headed Central War Industries Committee, 1915–17; plotted a palace *coup* against Nicholas II.

Kasso, Lev Aristidovich (1865–1914):   professor of law at the University of Moscow, 1898–1910; Acting Minister, then Minister of Education, 1910–1914; a hard-liner on issues of faculty autonomy and student rights.

Kokovtsev, Vladimir Nikolaevich (1853–1943):   career bureaucrat; Minister of Finance, 1904–05; helped negotiate French loan, 1906; Minister of Finance, 1906-14; Chairman of the Council of Ministers, 1911–1914.

Konovalov, Aleksandr Ivanovich (1875–1948):   prominent figure in Moscow commercial and industrial circles; leader of the Progressive Party in the Third Duma; one of the organizers of the Progressive Bloc, 1915; deputy chairman of the Central War Industries Committee, 1915–17.

Kuropatkin, General Aleksei Nikolaevich (1848–1925):   military commander; served on General Staff, 1898–1904; supporter of Russian expansion in the Far East; Commander of the Manchurian Army, 1904–March, 1905; relieved of his position after the battle of Mukden.

Lenin (b. Ulianov), Vladimir Ilyich (1870–1924):   revolutionary leader and Marxist propagandist; member of the editorial board of *Iskra*, 1900–03; author of *What Is To Be Done?* (1902); creator of the Bolshevik Party, 1903–05; lived abroad after 1907; returned to Petrograd, April, 1917.

Martov (b. Tsederbaum), Iulii Osipovich (1873–192?):   revolutionary leader and rival of Lenin in Marxist circles; broke with Lenin in 1903 and became leader of the Mensheviks in 1905; in exile, 1907–17.

Miliukov, Pavel Nikolaevich (1859–1943): historian at the University of Moscow; suspended in 1895 for encouraging student radicalism; prominent liberal and leader of the Constitutional Democratic Party; member of the Third and Fourth Dumas; helped to organize the Progressive Bloc in 1915.

Nicholas II (Nikolai Aleksandrovich) (1868–1918): second son of Alexander III, he became heir on the death of his older brother in 1865; as Tsarevich chaired committees on the Siberian railroad and on famine relief; crowned Tsar/Emperor, 1894; Commander-in-Chief of Russian forces, August 1915 – February 1917; abdicated 1917; executed 1918.

Nikolai Nikolaevich, Grand Duke (1856–1929): Inspector-General of Cavalry, 1895–1905; Commander of the St Petersburg Military District, 1904–14; Commander-in-Chief of Russian forces, July 1914 – August 1915; Commander of the Caucasian Army, 1915–17.

Plehve, Viacheslav Konstantinovich (1846–1904): career bureaucrat; Director of Police, 1881; Assistant Minister of the Interior, 1885; State-Secretary for the Grand Duchy of Finland, 1899; Minister of the Interior, 1902–04; assassinated by an SR terrorist.

Plekhanov, Georgii Valentinovich (1856–1918): historian and revolutionary theorist; founded the first Russian Marxist organization, the Emancipation of Labour group in Geneva, in 1883; member of the *Iskra* group, 1900–03; turned against Lenin's leadership after 1903.

Pobedonostsev, Konstantin Petrovich (1827–1907): statesman and legal scholar; tutor of both Alexander III and Nicholas II; as Procurator-General of the Holy Synod, 1880–1905, he opposed constitutional reform, parliamentary government, university autonomy, and the legalization of divorce.

Polivanov, Aleksei Andreevich (1855–1920): military commander; Assistant Minister of War, 1906–12; first Acting Minister, then Minister of War, 1914–16; opposed Nicholas II's decision to take command of the army and favoured negotiations with the Progressive Bloc; dismissed March, 1916.

Rasputin, Grigorii Efimovich (1871?–1916): a Siberian peasant from Pokrovskoe village in Tobolsk province; a *starets* or holy man who practiced an eccentric form of erotic spiritualism; from 1905, a favourite at the Russian Court who enjoyed a special relationship with the Tsarevich, a haemophiliac; murdered by right-wing conspirators, December, 1916.

Rediger, General Aleksandr Fedorovich (1853–1918): military commander, General of Infantry, 1907; Minister of War, 1905–09; military reformer who co-operated with Guchkov and the Third Duma; dismissed March, 1909 after Guchkov's attack on the competence of higher military officials, especially the Grand Dukes.

Riabushinskii, Pavel Pavlovich (1871–1924):   Moscow textile manufacturer, banker and political activist who in 1905 led the political awakening of the Moscow bourgeoisie; leader of the Moscow Progressives; led the campaign for the creation of war industries committees, 1915.

Rodzianko, Mikhail Vladimirovich (1859–1924):   a wealthy landowner from south Russia; prominent Octobrist member of the Third Duma; President of the Third Duma, 1911–12, and of the Fourth, 1912–17; took an active role during the 'munitions crisis' in 1915; pleaded for the appointment of a 'ministry of confidence', 1916–17.

Sergei Aleksandrovich, Grand Duke (1857–1905):   fourth son of Alexander II; Governor-General of Moscow, 1891 – January, 1905; Commander of the Moscow Military District, 1891 – February, 1905; an outspoken reactionary, he was blown to bits by a revolutionary bomb on 4 February, 1905.

Shcheglovitov, Ivan Grigorevich (1861–1918):   as Minister of Justice, 1906–15 and President of the State Council, he introduced field courts to suppress revolutionary terrorism; also actively involved in preparing the government's trumped-up case against Mendel Beilis in 1913.

Shipov, Dmitrii Nikolaevich (1851–1920):   board chairman of Moscow Provincial Zemstvo, 1893–1904; leader of the moderate zemstvo-constitutionalists in 1904–05; founder of the Union of 17 October (Octobrists); in late 1906 left to form the ineffectual Party of Peaceful Renovation.

Sipiagin, Dmitrii Sergeevich (1853–1902):   provincial governor; Assistant Minister of the Interior, 1894–95; Acting Minister of the Interior, 1899; Minister of the Interior, 1900–02; assassinated by an SR terrorist.

Stolypin, Petr Arkadevich (1862–1911):   provincial governor; Minister of the Interior, 1906 and Chairman of the Council of Ministers, 1906–11; a nationalist and strong monarchist, he attempted to co-operate with the Duma while introducing reforms to land tenure and local government; assassinated 1911.

Struve, Petr Berngardovich (1870–1944):   journalist and scholar, the archetypal intellectual in politics; until 1901, an ideologist of Marxism; turned to constitutional liberalism and became founding editor of *Osvobozhdenie (Liberation)*; joined Constitutional Democrats in 1905; organized the *Vekhi (Landmarks)* symposium of essays critical of the Russian intelligentsia.

Sviatopolk-Mirskii, Petr Danilovich (1857–1914): career bureaucrat; appointed Minister of the Interior, August, 1904; made an unsuccessful attempt to bridge the gap between the tsarist regime and the zemstvo leadership; dismissed in the wake of 'Bloody Sunday'.

Sukhomlinov, Vladimir Aleksandrovich (1848–1926): career military officer; General of Cavalry, 1906; Chief of General Staff, 1908; Minister of War, 1909–1915; subsequently arrested, impeached, and imprisoned for treason on account of his association with a convicted German spy.

Vyshnegradskii, Ivan Alekseevich (1830–1895): Minister of Finance, 1887–92; discredited by famine of 1891.

Witte, Sergei Iulevich (1849–1915): Minister of Transport, 1892; Minister of Finance, 1892–1903; driving spirit behind rapid industrialization and railway development; negotiated Treaty of Portsmouth, ending Russo-Japanese war; persuaded Nicholas II to issue October Manifesto, 1905; Chairman of the Council of Ministers, 1905–06; appointed to State Council, 1906–15.

Zubatov, Sergei Vasilevich (1864–1917): police official who sought to draw Russian workers away from social democracy; chief of the Moscow Okhrana (secret police), 1896–1902; dismissed from government service, 1903.

Map 1. European Russia

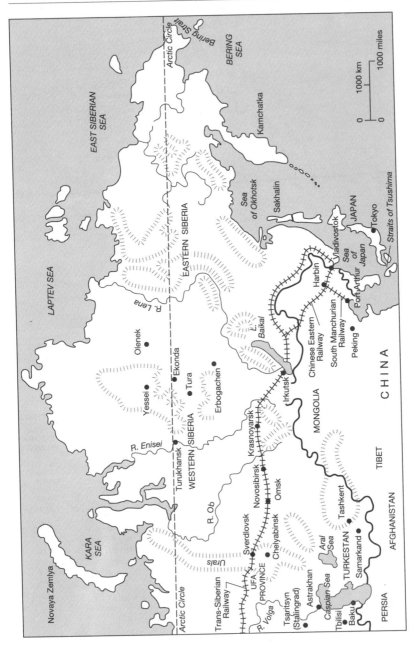

Map 2. Asiatic Russia

BIBLIOGRAPHY

PRINTED PRIMARY SOURCES

1 Bonnell, V.E. (ed.), *The Russian Worker. Life and Labor under the Tsarist Regime*, U of California Press, Berkeley, CA, 1983.

2 Cherniavsky, M. (ed. and trans.), *Prologue to Revolution. Notes of A.N. Iakhontov on the Secret Meetings of the Council of Ministers, 1915*, Prentice-Hall Inc., Englewood Cliffs, NJ, 1967.

3 Gurko, V.I., *Features and Figures of the Past: Government and Opinion in the Reign of Nicholas II*, Stanford UP, Stanford, CA, 1939.

4 [Guchkov, A.I.], 'Speech delivered by Mr A.I. Guchkov, on November 8, 1913, at the conference of the Octobrist party in St Petersburg. The general political situation and the Octobrist party' (trans. B. Pares), *Russian Review* III, No. 1 (1914), pp. 141–58.

5 Kirby, D.G. (ed. and trans.), *Finland and Russia 1808–1920: From Autonomy to Independence. A Selection of Documents*, Macmillan, London, 1975.

6 Maklakov, V.A., *The First State Duma: Contemporary Reminiscences* (trans. M. Belkin), Indiana U P, Bloomington, IN, 1964.

7 McCauley, M., *Octobrists to Bolsheviks: Imperial Russia 1905–1917*, Edward Arnold, London, 1984.

8 Miliukov, P., *Political Memoirs 1905–1917* (trans. C. Goldberg), ed. A.P. Mendel, U of Michigan Press, Ann Arbor, MI, 1967.

9 Ouroussof [Urusov], Prince S.D., *Mémoires d'un Gouverneur* (trans. S. Persky), Librairie Félix Juven, Paris, 1908.

10 Pobedonostsev, K.P., *Reflections of a Russian Statesman*, U of Michigan Press, Ann Arbor, MI, 1965.

11 Rodzianko, M.V., *The Reign of Rasputin: An Empire's Collapse* (trans. C. Zvegintzoff), A.M. Philpot Ltd., London, 1927.

12 Semyonova Tian-Shanskaia, O., *Village Life in Late Tsarist Russia*, ed. D.L. Ransel, Indiana U P, Bloomington, IN, 1993.

13 Shatz, M. and J.E. Zimmerman (eds. and trans.), *Vekhi/Landmarks: A Collection of Articles about the Russian Intelligentsia*, M.E. Sharpe Inc., Armonk, NY and London, 1994.

14 Shulgin, V.V., *Dni (Days)*, M.A. Suvorin, Belgrade, 1925.

15   Zelnik, R.E. (ed. and trans.), *A Radical Worker in Tsarist Russia: The Autobiography of Semën Ivanovich Kanatchikov*, Stanford UP, Stanford, CA, 1986.

SECONDARY SOURCES

16   Ascher, A., *The Revolution of 1905*, vol. 1, *Russia in Disarray*, Stanford U P, Stanford, CA, 1988.

17   Ascher, A., *The Revolution of 1905*, vol. 2, *Authority Restored*, Stanford U P, Stanford, CA, 1992.

18   Atkinson, D., 'The zemstvo and the peasantry', in T. Emmons and W.S.Vucinich (eds), *The Zemstvo in Russia: An Experiment in Local Self-Government*, Cambridge U P, Cambridge, 1982.

19   Balzer, H.D. (ed.), *Russia's Missing Middle Class. The Professions in Russian History*, M. E. Sharpe, Armonk, NY, 1996.

20   Bater, J.H., *St. Petersburg: Industrialization and Change*, McGill U P, Montreal, 1976.

21   Becker, S., *Nobility and Privilege in Late Imperial Russia*, Northern Illinois U P, DeKalb, IL, 1985.

22   Bonnell, V.E., *Roots of Rebellion: Workers' Politics and Organizations in St. Petersburg and Moscow, 1900–1914*, U of California Press, Berkeley and Los Angeles, CA, 1983.

23   Bradley, J., *Muzhik and Muscovite: Urbanization in Late Imperial Russia*, U of California Press, Berkeley and Los Angeles, CA, 1985.

24   Brooks, J., *When Russia Learned to Read: Literacy and Popular Literature, 1861–1917*, Princeton U P, Princeton, NJ, 1985.

25   Brower, D., 'Islam and ethnicity: Russian colonial policy in Turkestan', in D.R. Brower and E.J. Lazzerini (eds), *Russia's Orient. Imperial Borderlands and Peoples, 1700–1917*, Indiana UP, Bloomington and Indianapolis, IN, 1997.

26   Brower, D.R., *The Russian City between Tradition and Modernity, 1850–1900*, U of California Press, Berkeley, CA, 1990.

27   Bushnell, J., *Mutiny amid Repression: Russian Soldiers in the Revolution of 1905–1906*, Indiana U P, Bloomington, IN, 1985.

28   Byrnes, R.F., *Pobedonostsev: His Life and Thought*, Indiana U P, Bloomington, IN, 1968.

29   Clowes, E.W., S.D. Kassow and J.L. West (eds), *Between Tsar and People: Educated Society and the Quest for Public Identity in Late Imperial Russia*, Princeton U P, Princeton, NJ, 1991.

30   Edelman, R., *Gentry Politics on the Eve of the Russian Revolution*, Rutgers U P, New Brunswick, NJ, 1980.

31   Eklof, B., *Russian Peasant Schools: Officialdom, Village Culture and Popular Pedagogy, 1861–1914*, U of California Press, Berkeley and Los Angeles, CA, 1986.

32   Emmons, T., *The Formation of Political Parties and the First National Elections in Russia*, Harvard U P, Cambridge, MA, 1983.

33   Engelstein, L., *Moscow, 1905: Working-Class Organization and Political Conflict*, Stanford U P, Stanford, CA, 1982.

34   Fallows, T., 'The zemstvo and the bureaucracy, 1890–1904', in T. Emmons and W.S.Vucinich (eds), *The Zemstvo in Russia: An Experiment in Local Self-Government*, Cambridge U P, Cambridge, 1982.

35   Frank, S. P., 'Popular justice, community and culture among the Russian peasantry, 1870–1900', in B. Eklof and S. Frank (eds), *The World of the Russian Peasant*, Unwin Hyman Ltd., London, 1990.

36   Freeze, G.L., 'A national liberation movement and the shift in Russian liberalism, 1901–1903,' *Slavic Review*, 28, 1969.

37   Frieden, N.M., *Russian Physicians in an Era of Reform and Revolution, 1856–1905*, Princeton U P, Princeton, NJ, 1981.

38   Fuller, W.C. Jr., *Civil-Military Conflict in Imperial Russia, 1881–1914*. Princeton U P, Princeton, NJ, 1985.

39   Galai, S., *The Liberation Movement in Russia, 1900–1905*, Cambridge U P, Cambridge, 1973.

40   Gatrell, P., *The Tsarist Economy, 1850–1917*, Batsford, London, 1986.

41   Geyer, D., *The Russian Revolution* (trans. B. Little), Berg, Leamington Spa/Hamburg/New York, NY, 1987.

42   Gill, G.E., *Peasants and Government in the Russian Revolution*, Macmillan, London, 1979.

43   Gleason, W., *Alexander Guchkov and the End of the Russian Empire*, The American Philosophical Society, Philadelphia, PA, 1983.

44   Gleason, W., 'The all-Russian union of zemstvos and World War I', in T. Emmons and W.S.Vucinich (eds), *The Zemstvo in Russia: An Experiment in Local Self-Government*, Cambridge U P, Cambridge, 1982.

45   Glickman, R.L., *Russian Factory Women. Workplace and Society, 1880–1914*, U of California Press, Berkeley and Los Angeles, CA, and London, 1984.

46   Haimson, L.H. (ed.), *The Politics of Rural Russia, 1905–1914*, Indiana U P, Bloomington, IN, and London, 1979.

47   Haimson, L.H., 'The problem of social stability in urban Russia, 1905–1917', *Slavic Review*, 23–24, 1964–1965.

48   Hamburg, G.M., 'The crisis in Russian agriculture: a comment', *Slavic Review*, 37, 1978.

49   Hamm, M.F., *Kiev: A Portrait, 1800–1917*, Princeton U P, Princeton, NJ, 1993.

50   Healy, A.E., *The Russian Autocracy in Crisis 1905–1907*, Archon Books, Hampden, CT, 1976.

51   Herlihy, P., *Odessa: A History, 1794–1914*, Harvard Russian Research Institute, Cambridge, MA, 1986.

52   Hoch, S.L., 'On good numbers and bad: Malthus, population trends, and peasant standards of living in late Imperial Russia', *Slavic Review*, 53, 1994.

53   Hosking, G.A., *The Russian Constitutional Experiment: Government and Duma, 1907–1914*, Cambridge U P, Cambridge, 1973.

54   Hutchinson, J.F., *Politics and Public Health in Revolutionary Russia, 1890–1917*, Johns Hopkins U P, Baltimore, MD and London, 1990.

55   Johnson, R.E. 'Liberal professionals and professional liberals: the zemstvo statisticians and their work', in T. Emmons and W.S.Vucinich (eds), *The Zemstvo in Russia: An Experiment in Local Self-Government*, Cambridge U P, Cambridge, 1982.

56   Kassow, S., *Students, Professors and the State in Tsarist Russia*, U of California Press, Berkeley, CA, 1989.

57   Klier, John and S. Lambroza (eds), *Pogroms: Anti-Jewish Violence in Modern Russian History*, Cambridge U P, Cambridge, 1992.

58   Lincoln, W.B., *In War's Dark Shadow: The Russians Before the Great War*, Simon & Schuster, New York, NY, 1983.

59   Lindenmeyr, A., *Poverty Is Not a Vice: Charity, Society and the State in Imperial Russia*, Princeton U P, Princeton, NJ, 1996.

60   Lieven, D., *Nicholas II, Emperor of All the Russias*, John Murray, London, 1993; Random House Pimlico edition, 1994.

61   Lieven, D.C.B., *Russia and the Origins of the First World War*, St. Martin's Press, New York, NY, 1984.

62   Macey, D.A.J., *Government and Peasant in Russia: the Prehistory of the Stolypin Reforms*, Northen Illinois U P, De Kalb, IL, 1987.

63   Malozemoff, A., *Russian Far Eastern Policy, 1881–1904*, U of California Press, Berkeley and Los Angeles, CA, 1958.

64   Manning, R.T., *The Crisis of the Old Order in Russia: Gentry and Government*, Princeton U P, Princeton, NJ, 1982.

65   Manning, R.T., 'The zemstvo and politics, 1864–1914', in T. Emmons and W.S.Vucinich (eds), *The Zemstvo in Russia: An Experiment in Local Self-Government*, Cambridge U P, Cambridge, 1982.

66   Marks, S.G., *Road to Power: The Trans-Siberian Railroad and the Colonization of Asian Russia, 1850–1917*, Cornell U P, Ithaca, NY, 1991.

67   McDaniel, T., *Autocracy, Capitalism and Revolution in Russia*, U of California Press, Berkeley and Los Angeles, CA, 1988.

68   McDonald, D.M., *United Government and Foreign Policy in Russia 1900–1914*, Harvard U P, Cambridge, MA and London, 1992.

69   McKean, R. B., *St. Petersburg between the Revolutions: Workers and Revolutionaries, June 1907–February 1917*, Yale U P, New Haven, CT, 1990.

70   McReynolds, L., *The News under Russia's Old Regime: The Development of a Mass-Circulation Press*, Princeton U P, Princeton, NJ, 1991.

71   Mehlinger, H.D. and J.M. Thompson, *Count Witte and the Tsarist Government in the 1905 Revolution*, Indiana U P, Bloomington, IN, 1972.

72   Melancon, M., 'The Socialist Revolutionaries from 1902 to 1907: peasant *and* workers' party', *Russian History*, 12, 1985.

73 Nish, I., *The Origins of the Russo-Japanese War*, Longman, London and New York, NY, 1985.

74 Owen, T.C., *Capitalism and Politics in Russia. A Social History of the Moscow Merchants, 1855–1905*, Cambridge U P, Cambridge, London, and New York, NY, 1981.

75 Pares, B., *The Fall of the Russian Monarchy*, Knopf, New York, NY, 1939.

76 Patterson, K.D., 'Mortality in late tsarist Russia: a reconnaissance', *Social History of Medicine*, 8, 1995.

77 Pearson, R., *The Russian Moderates and the Crisis of Tsarism 1914–1917*, Macmillan, London and Basingstoke, 1977.

78 Perrie, M., *The Agrarian Policy of the Russian Socialist Revolutionary Party from its Origins to the Revolution of 1905–7*, Cambridge U P, Cambridge, 1976.

79 Pipes, R. (ed.), *Revolutionary Russia*, Harvard U P, Cambridge, MA, 1968.

80 Pipes, R., *Social Democracy and the St. Petersburg Labor Movement, 1885–1897*, Harvard U P, Cambridge, MA, 1963.

81 Pipes, R., *Struve: Liberal on the Left, 1870–1905*, Harvard U P, Cambridge, MA, 1970.

82 Pipes, R., *Struve: Liberal on the Right, 1905–1944*, Harvard U P, Cambridge, MA, 1980.

83 Pomper, P., *The Russian Revolutionary Intelligentsia*, 2nd ed. Harlan Davidson, Inc., Arlington Heights, IL, 1993.

84 Rabinowitch, A., *The Bolsheviks Come to Power. The Revolution of 1917 in Petrograd*, W.W. Norton, New York, NY, 1976.

85 Rawson, D.C., *Russian Rightists and the Revolution of 1905*, Cambridge U P, New York, NY, 1995.

86 Read, C., *Religion, Revolution and the Russian Intelligentsia, 1900–1912*, Macmillan, London, 1979.

87 Reichman, H., *Railwaymen and Revolution: Russia, 1905*, U of California Press, Berkeley, CA, 1987.

88 Rice, C., *Russian Workers and the Socialist-Revolutionary Party through the Revolution of 1905–1907*, Macmillan, New York, NY, 1988.

89 Rieber, A.J., *Merchants and Entrepreneurs in Imperial Russia*, U of North Carolina Press, Chapel Hill, NC, 1982.

90 Riha, T., *A Russian European. Paul Miliukov in Russian Politics*, Notre Dame U P, Notre Dame, IN, 1969.

91 Robbins, R.G., Jr., *Famine in Russia 1891–1892: The Imperial Government Responds to a Crisis*, Columbia U P, New York, NY, 1975.

92 Robbins, R.G., Jr., *The Tsar's Viceroys: Russian Provincial Governors in the Last Years of the Empire*, Cornell U P, Ithaca, NY, 1987.

93 Rogger, H., *Jewish Policies and Right-Wing Politics in Imperial Russia*, U of California Press, Berkeley, CA, 1986.

94 Rogger, H., *Russia in the Age of Modernization and Revolution, 1881–1917*, Longman, London and New York, NY, 1983.

95   Rosenberg, W.G., 'The zemstvo in 1917 and under Bolshevik rule', in
      T. Emmons and W.S.Vucinich (eds), *The Zemstvo in Russia: An
      Experiment in Local Self-Government*, Cambridge U P, Cambridge,
      1982.

96   Ruckman, J.A., *The Moscow Business Elite: A Social and Cultural Por-
      trait of Two Generations, 1840–1905*, Northern Illinois U P, DeKalb,
      IL, 1984.

97   Sablinsky, W., *The Road to Bloody Sunday: Father Gapon and the St.
      Petersburg Massacre of 1905*, Princeton U P, Princeton, NJ, 1976.

98   Schneidermann, J., *Sergei Zubatov and Revolutionary Marxism: The
      Struggle for the Working Class in Tsarist Russia*, Cornell U P, Ithaca
      and London, 1976.

99   Seregny, S.J., *Russian Teachers and Peasant Revolution. The Politics of
      Education in 1905*, Indiana U P, Bloomington and Indianapolis, IN,
      1989.

100   Seton-Watson, H., *The Russian Empire 1801–1917*, Clarendon Press,
      Oxford, 1967.

101   Shanin, T., *Russia as a 'Developing Society'*, Macmillan, London,
      1985.

102   Siegelbaum, L.H., *The Politics of Industrial Mobilization in Russia,
      1915–1917: A Study of the War-Industries Committees*, St. Martin's
      Press, New York, NY, 1984.

103   Simms, J.Y., 'The crisis in Russian agriculture at the end of the nine-
      teenth century: a different view', *Slavic Review*, 36, 1977.

104   Sinel, A.A., *The Classroom and the Chancellery: State Educational
      Reform in Russia under Count Dmitrii Tolstoi*, Harvard U P, Cam-
      bridge, MA, 1973.

105   Skinner, F.W., 'Odessa and the problem of urban modernization', in
      M.F. Hamm (ed.), *The City in Late Imperial Russia*, Indiana U P,
      Bloomington, IN, 1986.

106   Steinberg, J.W., 'Russian General Staff training and the approach of
      war', in F. Coetzee and M. Shevin-Coetzee (eds), *Authority, Identity
      and the Social History of the Great War*, Berghahn Books, Provi-
      dence, RI and Oxford, 1995.

107   Stone, N., *The Eastern Front, 1914–1917*, Hodder and Stoughton,
      London, 1975.

108   Suny, R.G., 'Toward a social history of the October Revolution', *Amer-
      ican Historical Review*, 88, 1983.

109   Surh, G.D., *1905 in St. Petersburg: Labor, Society, and Revolution*,
      Stanford U P, Stanford, CA, 1989.

110   Thaden, E.C., *Conservative Nationalism in Nineteenth-Century Russia*,
      U of Washington Press, Seattle, 1964.

111   Thaden, E.C., *Russification in the Baltic Provinces and Finland, 1855–
      1914*, Princeton U P, Princeton, NJ, 1981.

112   Thurston, R.W., *Liberal City, Conservative State: Moscow and Rus-
      sia's Urban Crisis, 1906–1914*, Oxford U P, New York, NY, 1987.

113 Verner, A., *The Crisis of Russian Autocracy: Nicholas II and the 1905 Revolution*, Princeton U P, Princeton, NJ, 1990.

114 von Laue, T.H., *Sergei Witte and the Industrialization of Russia*, Columbia U P, New York, NY, and London, 1963.

115 Weissman, N.B., *Reform in Tsarist Russia. The State Bureaucracy and Local Government, 1900–1914*, Rutgers U P, New Brunswick, NJ, 1981.

116 West, J.L., 'The Riabushinskii circle: *burzhuaziia* and *obshchestvennost'* in late Imperial Russia', in E.W. Clowes, S.D. Kassow and J.L. West (eds), *Between Tsar and People: Educated Society and the Quest for Public Identity in Late Imperial Russia*, Princeton U P, Princeton, NJ., 1991.

117 Wildman, A., *The Making of a Workers' Revolution: Russian Social Democracy, 1891–1903*, U of Chicago Press, Chicago, IL, 1967.

118 Yaney, G.L., *The Systematization of Russian Government: Social Evolution in the Domestic Administration of Imperial Russia, 1711–1905*, U of Illinois Press, Urbana, IL, 1973.

119 Yaroshevski, D., 'Empire and citizenship', in D.R. Brower and E.J. Lazzerini (eds), *Russia's Orient: Imperial Borderlands and Peoples, 1700–1917*, Indiana U P, Bloomington and Indianapolis, IN, 1997.

120 Zaionchkovskii, P.A., *The Russian Autocracy in Crisis, 1878–1882* (trans. G. M. Hamburg), Academic International Press, Gulf Breeze, FL, 1979.

INDEX